THE GOAL
AND
THE GLORY

America's Athletes
Speak Their Faith

Edited by
TED SIMONSON

FLEMING H. REVELL COMPANY

The Scripture quotations marked RSV in this publication are from the *Revised Standard Version of the Bible,* copyrighted 1946 and 1952 by the Division of Christian Education, National Council of Churches, and used by permission.

The Scripture quotations marked PHILLIPS in this publication are from *The New Testament in Modern English,* © J. B. Phillips 1958. Used by permission of The Macmillan Company.

The picture of Wilma Rudolph is a *New York Daily News* photograph.

To LOUIS H. EVANS
*Founding Father and Honorary Trustee
of the Fellowship of Christian Athletes*

INTRODUCTION

THIS IS a book of devotions written by some of the most talented athletes in America today. Nearly all of them I know personally. I can vouch for their dedication. However, the number of testimonies here is far from complete. They have been selected to insure representation of all major sports, both college and professional athletes, and coaches as well as players, but their number could be multiplied many times across the land in athletes who freely confess their allegiance to Christ and serve Him in His Church.

The sports personalities in this book and many others today are associated with the Fellowship of Christian Athletes. FCA is a movement to confront athletes—and through them, the youth of the nation—with the challenge and adventure of following Christ in the fellowship of the Church. This book is one way in which this challenge is being presented.

A careful reading of the following devotional thoughts may surprise you. Certainly it will blast forever the lie that religion is something soft and fragile, an occupation for delicate temperaments.

Those who have written these selections have embraced rigorous discipline and severe bodily punishment as a regular way of life. They compete day after day with the finest physically equipped athletes in the world today. They stay on top by putting 100 per cent of their effort into every jump-up, every turn at bat, every time the center snaps the ball. Besides this, they work in a business in which muscles have dollar signs on them and where fans can make a boy a hero overnight.

In spite of these things, these people confess a common belief that a Man crucified nearly 2000 years ago still lives.

And if such forthright testimonies can be found in the tough, competitive world of professional athletics, it should be clear that Jesus Christ has something to offer everybody—everywhere!

BRANCH RICKEY

CONTRIBUTORS

FELIPE ALOU

Outstanding outfielder from the Dominican Republic; currently with Milwaukee Braves. Advisory Council, Fellowship of Christian Athletes.

RAYMOND BERRY

Versatile end Southern Methodist University; currently All-Pro end with Baltimore Colts. Advisory Council, Fellowship of Christian Athletes.

FRANK BROYLES

Halfback Georgia Tech; head coach Missouri University. Currently head football coach Arkansas University where teams have been Conference and Holiday Bowl Champions; winner 1965 Cotton Bowl and voted 1964 Coach-of-the-Year. Advisory Council, Fellowship of Christian Athletes.

ALVIN DARK

All-Star shortstop Boston Braves; team captain New York Giants; former manager pennant champions San Francisco Giants; currently coach Chicago Cubs. Advisory Council, Fellowship of Christian Athletes.

DON DEMETER

Outfielder Los Angeles Dodgers, currently with Detroit Tigers. Advisory Council, Fellowship of Christian Athletes.

BUDDY DIAL

All-American football Rice Institute, currently end with Dallas Cowboys. Advisory Council, Fellowship of Christian Athletes.

PAUL DIETZEL

Outstanding lineman Miami University of Ohio, "1958 Coach of the Year" Louisiana State University, currently head football coach at United States Military Academy. Board of Directors, Fellowship of Christian Athletes.

GIL DODDS

World champion miler, Boston Athletic Association; currently involved in youth work, and counselor, Naperville Community High School, Naperville, Illinois.

CARL ERSKINE

All-Star and World Series pitching ace, Brooklyn and Los Angeles Dodgers, pitched two no-hit no-run games; held World Series strike-out record of 14 against Yankees. Currently in insurance business in Anderson, Indiana. Advisory Council, Fellowship of Christian Athletes.

DAVE FERRISS

Twenty-five game winner and pitching coach Boston Red Sox. Currently athletic director, Delta State College, Cleveland, Mississippi.

BILL GLASS

Outstanding football player Baylor University, defensive end, Cleveland Browns. Advisory Council, Fellowship of Christian Athletes.

OTTO GRAHAM

All-American football Northwestern University; All-Pro "Mr. Quarterback" Cleveland Browns; currently coach College All-Stars and athletic director U.S. Coast Guard Academy. Advisory Council, Fellowship of Christian Athletes.

RAFER JOHNSON

World's greatest athlete holding World and Olympic records in decathlon track events; currently assistant track coach U.C.L.A., and People-to-People staff. Advisory Council, Fellowship of Christian Athletes.

ROE H. JOHNSTON

All-American football Navy. Currently pastor of a Presbyterian Church, San Francisco, California. Honorary Trustee, Fellowship of Christian Athletes.

JERRY KINDALL

All-American baseball University of Minnesota. Currently second baseman Minnesota Twins.

BILL KRISHER

All-American football Oklahoma University; All-Pro guard Dallas Texans; currently Associate Director, Fellowship of Christian Athletes.

8

VERNON LAW

All-Star, World Series ace pitcher Pittsburgh Pirates; winner of 1960 Cy Young Award as outstanding pitcher in baseball. Advisory Council, Fellowship of Christian Athletes.

DONN MOOMAW

All-American football U.C.L.A. "Lineman of the Year" award 1952 and All-Canadian football; College Football "Hall of Fame;" currently pastor Presbyterian Church, Los Angeles, California. Board of Directors, Fellowship of Christian Athletes.

C. L. "BIGGIE" MUNN

All-American football Minnesota; "1951 Coach of the Year" Michigan State University; currently athletic director Michigan State University. Board of Directors, Fellowship of Christian Athletes.

JACK PARR

All-American basketball Kansas State University; professional Cincinnati Royals; currently in sports equipment business in Salina, Kansas. Advisory Council, Fellowship of Christian Athletes.

BOB PETTIT

All-American basketball Louisiana State University; currently All-Pro St. Louis Hawks and all-time leading scorer. Advisory Council, Fellowship of Christian Athletes.

JOHN "BUBBA" PHILLIPS

Third baseman with 1960 American League Champion Chicago White Sox; currently third baseman with Detroit Tigers.

BOBBY RICHARDSON

All-Star second baseman New York Yankees; "The Mouse That Roared" drove in record 12 runs during 1960 World Series. Advisory Council, Fellowship of Christian Athletes.

BRANCH RICKEY

Father of modern baseball; developer of World Championship teams in St. Louis, Brooklyn and Pittsburgh; currently retired. Chairman, Honorary Trustees, Fellowship of Christian Athletes.

9

BROOKS ROBINSON

All-Star third baseman Baltimore Orioles; 1964 Most Valuable Player in American League.

WILMA RUDOLPH

All-American track Tennessee A & I College. World and Olympic track champion. Currently teacher Tennessee.

JIM RAY SMITH

All-American football Baylor University. Currently All-Pro guard Dallas Cowboys. Advisory Council, Fellowship of Christian Athletes.

FRANCIS TARKENTON

All-American football and honor student University of Georgia; quarterback Minnesota Vikings; most outstanding player 1965 All-Star game. Advisory Council, Fellowship of Christian Athletes.

CLENDON THOMAS

All-American football Oklahoma University; led nation in scoring 1956. Currently All-Pro halfback Pittsburgh Steelers.

DAN TOWLER

All-American football Washington and Jefferson; All-Pro leading ground-gaining fullback in Los Angeles Rams history; currently a pastor in Pasadena, California. Board of Directors, Fellowship of Christian Athletes.

BILL WADE

Outstanding football player Vanderbilt University; broke all-time passing mark of Los Angeles Rams, 1959; WLAC—TV Sports Announcer; currently quarterback Chicago Bears. Advisory Council, Fellowship of Christian Athletes.

CONTENTS

CONTENTS

I

"SUITING UP"

Becoming a Christian

BOBBY RICHARDSON

Commitment

(For there is no distinction to be made anywhere: everyone has sinned, everyone has fallen short of the beauty of God's plan.) Under this divine "system" a man who has faith is now freely acquitted in the eyes of God by His generous dealing in the Redemptive Act of Jesus Christ. God has appointed Him as the means of propitiation, a propitiation accomplished by the shedding of His blood, to be received and made effective in ourselves by faith. God has done this to demonstrate His Righteousness both by the wiping out of the sins of the past (the time when He withheld His Hand), and by showing in the present time that He is a just God and that He justifies every man who has faith in Jesus Christ. ROMANS 3:23-26 (PHILLIPS)

. . . him that cometh to me I will in no wise cast out. JOHN 6:37 (PHILLIPS)

I BECAME A Christian when I was twelve years old. Our pastor had visited our home several times and talked with me about Christ. And during one of his visits, we knelt in prayer and I asked the Lord to take over my life. On the following Sunday in church I publicly announced my commitment.

Some people feel that there is no need to make such an issue of this decision. But I feel that commitment is a contract made between a person and God and the more definite it is, the better.

15

When my wife and I decided to spend the rest of our lives together, we invited everybody we knew to come and witness our marriage vows. In essence, we gave ourselves to each other.

When I was offered the opportunity to play baseball for the Yankees, the first thing we did was sign a contract. I agreed to play for no other club, while the Yankees promised me a certain salary and other benefits. In other words, I gave my baseball talents to the Yankees for a specified time and, in exchange, the Yankee organization gave itself to me in terms of club membership and its privileges.

There's a certain parallel to the commitment a man makes to God when he becomes a Christian. In a very real sense, he gives himself to Christ and Christ gives Himself in return. The only difference in this contract is that the man has eternity to gain and nothing to lose but his sins. The Bible teaches that ". . . all have sinned and come short of the glory of God" (Romans 3:28). All of us are evil in nature and helpless in our own strength to do anything about it. We need a Saviour.

On the cross, Jesus voluntarily suffered the punishment that each of us deserves for sins committed. And in seeing the cross in this light and accepting His sacrifice in our behalf, we receive forgiveness and a new life.

It's important to understand that His forgiveness comes to us freely. We will never fully understand it. We don't deserve it. And we certainly can do nothing to earn it. "For by grace are ye saved through faith; and that not of yourselves: it is the gift of God: Not of works, lest any man should boast" (Ephesians 2:8,9).

When someone fully understands this and offers himself to God on this basis, it remains for God to confirm the contract. And He does. "The Spirit itself beareth witness with our spirit, that we are the children of God" (Romans 8:16). This promised confirmation by God makes the "contract" definite. And we should be grateful for it. Besides sensing a need for a Saviour and trusting in Him, we can actually experience the change of heart within and know for certain that our new life is genuine.

One further word. We need to recommit ourselves to Christ day by day. I had to learn this the hard way.

Although I had become a Christian at the age of twelve, baseball began to command a larger and larger part of my life in the years that followed. On a Salvation Army youth team, Little League and on into American Legion baseball, my devotion to the game continued to grow.

When I signed with the Yankee farm system at the age of seventeen, I was the happiest kid in the world. But I wasn't prepared for the long, tough, lonely struggle that would follow.

In reporting to my first training camp, I'll never forget the Greyhound bus pulling into Norfolk, Virginia, in the cold, grey dawn of June, 1953. Left behind were all my friends and supporters. Ahead was a big skeptical world that had seen many a local star fall flat on his face.

As discouragement set in during those first few days, a note arrived from my home-town coach, Conley Alexander, and in it he quoted Matthew 6:33: ". . . seek ye first the kingdom of God, and his righteousness; and all these things shall be added unto you."

With a sense of shame, I remembered that first and

17

foremost I was a Christian. I began to believe then that God had put me in baseball for a purpose, to glorify Him.

And this led me to a recommitment of my life.

Later I ran into Johnny Hunton, an outstanding Christian in A and Double A baseball. His tremendous courage in standing up for Christ in professional baseball was a great inspiration. I wanted to be just as faithful in my discipleship.

Once again I confirmed my original commitment to Christ. When I was dropped back to D baseball and thought my days in the sport were numbered, He held me steady. Now I commit my life anew to Him at the beginning of each day, often before each game.

It's not because the old commitment "runs out" like a baseball contract. It's because it is strengthening to remember in the midst of constantly changing circumstances that I have a great, unchanging Lord.

Prayer

Dear Lord, I come to Thee with empty hands. I cannot recommend myself. I am in need of forgiveness. But daring to believe the mighty promises of Thy word, I offer myself to Thee in the name of Thy Son, Jesus Christ. I believe that Thou wilt accept me on this basis and give me a new life as His disciple. Confirm this contract by Thy Spirit as I commit this day into Thy keeping. I ask it in Jesus' name. Amen.

BILL KRISHER

A Purpose for Life

> . . . so now also Christ shall be magnified in my body, whether it be by life, or by death. For to me to live is Christ, and to die is gain. PHILIPPIANS 1:20-21

WHAT ARE YOU living for?

Maybe you'll have a hard time answering that question honestly. I know it took something special in my life to make me dig for an answer.

I was a freshman at Oklahoma University and a second-string guard on the football team when a serious knee injury put me flat on my back. After the operation, the doctor told me, "Bill, three ligaments and a cartilage have been pretty well mutilated. I'm afraid you won't be able to play any more ball."

After the doctor left my hospital room, I looked up at the ceiling and began thinking. I'd played football since eighth grade. What would my life be like without it? What would it be like sitting on the sidelines watching the others blocking, tackling, running with the ball?

What was I living for anyway?

Plenty of people I'd met were living quite frankly for *pleasure*. But this is asking no more of life than an animal asks. And the Bible teaches that man is created in the image of God. There is eternity in him and he can

19

have fellowship with the Almighty. Living only for pleasure makes it impossible for him to enjoy God's presence in this life and leaves him completely unprepared for the greater fellowship that is possible in the next.

Many people live for *material security*. Job interviewers contacting college seniors these days are being surprised. The old questions about salary and the chances for advancement are being pushed aside for a new question that is being asked quite sincerely: "What kind of retirement plan does your company offer?"

Today's concern with material security is especially ironic because no generation in history before this one has grown up with the threat of world-wide nuclear destruction. Actually there is no such thing as material security. There never has been. Death comes to all of us, young and old. And all the bank accounts and stocks and bonds in the world cannot change this fact for anyone.

Still others live for *success in their chosen vocation.* A familiar sight to pro football players each summer is the incoming rookie. Many youngsters, of course, are fine fellows. But there are always a few who come into the club ready to tear up the world. They've got their press clippings and trophies packed in their suitcases and they are ready to claw and scramble and promote themselves to the top of the heap as soon as possible. Boys who may never before have taken a drink or been promiscuous are now ready to throw away their scruples for a chance to get in with the "right" clique. Compromise is the order of the day.

But even if this kind of personal promotion were to pay off (which it usually doesn't!) what is the best "success" such a ball player can hope for? Eight or ten years of pro action? Then what? It's all over and character has been sacrificed.

What do we mean by "success" anway? Success by whose standards? The Bible teaches that God is the final Judge before whom we shall all stand one day. God then will proclaim us "successful" or "unsuccessful."

What is *your* goal in life? Do you have one strong purpose for living? If not, ponder this: people who aim at nothing in particular usually achieve just that.

Paul said, "For me to live is Christ." I came to the same conclusion as I lay on that hospital bed after my knee operation. I decided to live completely for Christ. I knew I could serve Him with a broken knee or, for that matter, with no knee at all. He had died for my sins, granted me fellowship with Himself, given me assurance about the life to come. Why *shouldn't* I live for Him?

My knee injury did not spell the end of my football career however. After months of exercise, the injured tissue responded enough to permit a walk, then a limping run, finally a full sprint. Today, thanks to His grace, I'm still playing football!

Prayer Suggestion

Give your life an "agonizing reappraisal." If you're not sure about the direction in which you're going, ask God to clear away the confusion. Ask Him to show you what's wrong and how to set it right. Dare to believe that you could be a twentieth-century disciple of Jesus Christ.

BILL GLASS

God's Gift

> But even though we were dead in our sins God was so
> rich in mercy that He gave us the very life of Christ (for
> it is, remember, by grace and not by achievement that you
> are saved), and has lifted us right out of the old life to
> take our place with Him in Christ in the heavens. Thus He
> shows for all time the tremendous generosity of the grace
> and kindness He has expressed towards us in Christ Jesus.
> It was nothing you could or did achieve—it was God's gift
> to you. EPHESIANS 2:4-8 (PHILLIPS)

EVERYWHERE YOU LOOK in life, you see a certain law in
operation. This law is "hard work gets results." Ask the
millionaire how he piled up so much money and his
answer will be "Hard work!" Ask the successful farmer,
mechanic, businessman how they did it and their answers will probably be the same.

You can see this law operating in athletics. All my
sports' life—in junior high, high school, college and in
professional football—I've heard the same basic advice:
you can't be an effective athlete if you don't work hard.

"They're not going to give you the game! You've just
got to go out there and take it away from them!"

Perhaps this is the reason athletes as well as most
other people find it so difficult to understand the
Christian faith. Hard work, discipline and teamwork are

values anyone can understand easily and admire. But in the most important transaction of your life, hard work is your worst enemy, discipline will not help and team-work is impossible!

"It is, remember, by grace and not by achievement that you are saved."

The law of self-achievement becomes completely worthless when we seek a relationship with God. He is not an impersonal employer who pays us for our serv-ices. He is a holy and righteous God before whom we stand in our sin, condemned and guilty. We cannot work our way out of this dilemma. Our so-called "good" efforts are shot through with self-interest and our sin multiplies even as we struggle to be virtuous.

I was sixteen and a junior in high school in Corpus Christi, Texas, when I began to realize how impossible it was to work my way into God's favor. I had gone to church occasionally in the past, but now I made it a point to attend regularly. I watched Christian fellows and girls I admired and tried to copy them. But it was difficult and never successful. I could fool other people for a short time but I could never fool myself.

All my efforts to be good only seemed to pull me further from God. I felt like a hypocrite. I knew the whole thing was an act.

Then, during a church service one Sunday morning, I realized that I'd been going at it all wrong. I saw my-self as a helpless sinner with nothing to offer in my own defense. I realized that as I came to Christ in this way and trusted Him as Saviour, He would give me freely the forgiveness and peace of mind I had worked so hard to "earn."

I finally came to see salvation for what it was—a gift. You can't "pay" for a gift. All you can do is accept it and say "Thank you." It's a simple and humbling experience. I guess that's why so many people miss it.

When I was playing football with Baylor University, the fullback, a Christian, presented this truth to one of the other team members one day in the locker room.

"I know I need to face my need for God," the other boy said, "but I'll do it later."

As he turned to leave the room, the fullback said, "What's the matter? No guts?"

These words stopped the other boy in his tracks. He came back to talk some more about it. And that day he became a Christian.

Strange to say, it takes more courage to come to God emptyhanded, confessing your sin, than to approach Him in the proud consciousness of your "achievements."

And this humble position before Him never changes! We are *continually* in need of the grace of God as provided in Jesus Christ. And it continues true that we cannot "earn" it or "work" for it. It is given freely.

We may be tempted to forget this when we have experienced a setback. When a Christian sins, the devil mocks him, accuses him of hypocrisy and advises him to take a seat on the sidelines. But the wise Christian goes immediately to his Master, admitting his failure and asking forgiveness.

". . . if we freely admit that we have sinned, we find God utterly reliable and straightforward—He forgives our sins and makes us thoroughly clean from all that is evil" (I John 1:9, PHILLIPS). Following his frank confession, the Christian is immediately reinstated and is back in action, doing God's will.

I have studied films taken of defensive football plays most of my life. And I have discovered that 75 per cent of all tackles made are made by men who seem, at one point, to be out of action. But these men have refused to stay down. They have gotten to their feet again and made the critical tackle.

Spiritually you may be knocked down. It may seem that everything has gone wrong. But Christ still loves you. And in that dark moment He forgives and gives you new strength. You get to your feet and find victory.

The secret is seeing God as the great Gift-giver and Jesus Christ as the greatest of His gifts.

Prayer

Heavenly Father, I am through making apologies for myself. I admit my sinful condition. I am ready now to recognize Thy Son Jesus as my only resource and to believe I am received and forgiven through Him as a free gift of Thy grace. I thank Thee in His name. Amen.

BROOKS ROBINSON

Sin

But God shows his love for us in that while we were yet sinners Christ died for us. ROMANS 5:8 (RSV)

THERE ARE PLENTY of temptations in professional baseball. I suppose there are temptations no matter where you work. But in baseball you travel a great deal. You never stay long in one place. While you're on the road, you put up in a different hotel every week, eat in different restaurants, even go to a different church every Sunday.

You're away from the security and familiarity of your home and family. And you have a lot of free time. This gives the devil a lot to work with. And he does just that. Many men have wrecked their characters and their lives by playing fast and loose on the road.

Before I became a Christian, I knew when I sinned and I regretted it. I've been brought up in a church-going family. I had principles and I was aware when they were violated. But it didn't bother me too much. But as a Christian, things are different. When I commit a sin, there's nothing casual about how I feel. I'm not simply violating a self-created "code of honor." I know now that I am sinning against the One who gave His life for me on the cross.

Someone has said that the closer we get to Christ, the more conscious we are of sin. I believe this is true.

In an old comic strip, Andy Gump tells his son Chester that he's been disobeying too much. To make his point, he puts up a post in the back yard and tells Chester he will drive a nail into the post for each disobedience.

When the post is just about covered with nails, Chester adopts a new attitude. Andy then begins to pull out a nail each time his son obeys him. When the last nail is drawn, he calls Chester to see the post. But Chester begins to cry.

"What's the matter?" Andy asks in surprise.

"The scars are still there," the boy answers.

That's one of the disagreeable things about sin. It leaves a person feeling scarred.

I imagine that's the way the prodigal son felt when he finally came to his senses far from home and with all his money gone. Fortunately he adopted a humble attitude. He came to his father with a full confession, admitting that he had given up his right to be called a son.

Many people fail to take this attitude when they have violated God's commandments. Instead they feel proud and defiant. "Why should I get down on my knees and grovel before God?" they ask. "There are plenty of people worse than I am!"

Pride is probably the thing that causes us to sin the most. Just take the matter of receiving credit for something. When we do something outstanding, we naturally want recognition. We accept it gladly. And if it doesn't come or it goes to someone else, we feel deflated. And yet Jesus said to His followers, "Without me, ye can do nothing." This means that anything worthwhile we may

27

accomplish, we accomplish in His strength and under His direction. And it should be for His glory, not ours. Small wonder when we grab praise for ourselves rightfully belonging to Him that we find ourselves unable to ward off temptation!

But the best part of the story of the prodigal son takes place when he gets back home. His father runs to meet him with joy. While the young man is making his confession, his father is shouting to the servants to bring the best clothes and a ring for his finger. A great celebration is ordered.

This story was told by Jesus to illustrate how joyfully God forgives us when we approach Him in humility. How can we be too proud to do this when Jesus went to the cross on our behalf? Hasn't He done as much as He could to convince us of His father's love and mercy?

Can you honestly say about your own past, "Father, I have done wrong in the sight of heaven and in your eyes. I don't deserve to be called your son any more"? If you can, and if you can see that God through Christ is ready to forgive you, you stand on the threshold of a new life.

Prayer

Dear Lord, like the prodigal son, I confess my sin and come before Thee with no excuses. I present nothing but my faith in Thy Son. Forgive as Thou hast promised. I ask it in Jesus' name. Amen.

FELIPE ALOU

Finding Christ

> Let not mercy and truth forsake thee: bind them about thy
> neck; write them upon the table of thine heart: So shalt
> thou find favour and good understanding in the sight of
> God and man. Trust in the Lord with all thine heart; and
> lean not to thine own understanding. In all thy ways ac-
> knowledge him, and he shall direct thy paths. Be not wise
> in thine own eyes: fear the Lord, and depart from evil.
> PROVERBS 3:3-7

I AM A Christian today because of the faithfulness of a
friend. His name is Roque Martinez—we went to school
together in the Dominican Republic. In those days all
I thought about was baseball and my dream of becoming a big league player.

Roque secured a job in Canada in 1954. When he
came back a year or two later, he told me he had gone to
a church in Canada and become a believer. I was glad
to see him after his long absence, but I was a bit em-
barrassed by his new enthusiasm. Religion for me was
going to church and keeping out of trouble. But not
much more.

In 1956 my break came and I went to Florida to play
in the state league there. Before I left, Roque gave me
a Spanish Bible and told me to read it. Because I had

29

promised, I did read it. But it was like a story about someone else—not something real.

During the next two years, I played baseball with all my heart. My one ambition was to reach the top. It was all I lived for.

Each time I came home to the Dominican Republic for the winter season, my friend was waiting. Each time he would tell me that he had been praying for me. And each time he would ask me if I had become a Christian.

I had deep affection for Roque and appreciated his prayers. But how could I tell him that baseball, not religion, was the important thing in my life? Another thing made it hard for me to be frank. As a concrete worker in the Dominican Republic, Roque made barely enough to live on. And by contrast, as a minor league baseball player in the United States, I was living like a king.

Then, in June of 1958 the news came that I had been waiting a lifetime for. I was playing Triple A ball in Seattle, Washington, when the Giants notified me that I would be flown down to San Francisco the next day to play my first major league game. I was being moved up to the majors at last!

At the same time a telegram came to me from Roque. In it he said that he had prayed two things: that I would become a big league player; and that before I played my first major league game, I would become a Christian. In the same telegram he mentioned Proverbs 3:3-7. I opened my Bible and read, "Be not wise in thine own eyes: fear the Lord, and depart from evil."

Oddly enough, it was not the truth of this passage that so deeply affected me at this time. It was the knowledge of how much in actual cash that long telegram must have cost my poor friend in the far-off

Caribbean! In spite of the hardship and privation of his life, he had sent an expensive telegram 3000 miles to a friend to tell him about a prayer!

I flew down to San Francisco, but it rained and the game was postponed one day. I spent most of that rainy day in my hotel room staring at that telegram. Then at last, I got down on my knees and gave myself to the Lord.

The next day, June 8, 1958, I played my first game as a major leaguer—and as a Christian.

Roque's prayers had been answered.

During the next few days, so new in the faith and with so many questions, I hardly knew where to turn. But God led me to Al Worthington, a pitcher for the Giants. And Al helped me and answered many of my questions.

I wrote home right away to my friends and relatives, telling them of my conversion. And when I returned home that winter, I told everyone I could about my new life in Christ. I found out, of course, that not everyone wishes to hear about Christ. I experienced ridicule and misunderstanding. But in His strength I held on and maintained my testimony, until my friends became convinced that I was not pretending.

Time passes swiftly. Life is short. The time when I will die is coming soon. I want to be ready.

I want to live right in the meantime as well. Each day I pray that I will keep my temper and behave like a Christian, so that the players and fans will know my true purpose.

Before I became a Christian, I worried about many things. When I went into a batting slump, I was sick about it. Now I wait patiently for my average to come up again. I used to worry about traveling in airplanes. Now I trust Him with each trip.

But this trust is nothing I can boast about. I would know nothing at all about it if a Christian friend had not been faithful.

Prayer

Dear Lord, Thank you for friends in the faith who care and pray and witness. Help me to be such a friend to those who know me. I ask it in Jesus' name. Amen.

RAYMOND BERRY

The Changed Life

> For God so loved the world that he gave his only Son, that whoever believes in him should not perish but have eternal life. JOHN 3:16 (RSV)

> . . . Now this he [Jesus] said about the Spirit, which those who believed in him were to receive. . . . JOHN 7:39 (RSV)

> But you are not in the flesh, you are in the Spirit, if the Spirit of God really dwells in you. Anyone who does not have the Spirit of Christ does not belong to him. But if Christ is in you, although your bodies are dead because of sin, your spirits are alive because of righteousness. ROMANS 8:9-10 (RSV)

WHEN I WAS a young boy, I attended Sunday school and church regularly, and at about the age of twelve, I was baptized. I believed this about Jesus: He was the Son of God who was put to death on a cross and was raised from the dead on the third day. It never entered my mind then or during the next fifteen years to ask questions like these:

Why was Jesus sent by God? What did His life, death and resurrection mean? Why was He put to death on a cross? Why is He referred to as "Saviour"? And how does this concern me?

I continued to be a churchgoer during high school,

33

college and after college, but I remained in darkness concerning the good news of the gospel. I was very aware of the existence of God, mainly because of the many blessings He bestowed on my life. But when I prayed, there was no mention of Christ's name. Jesus just wasn't "real" to me. I didn't know Him or know of Him.

I read the Bible just enough to know that there was such a thing as "sin" and a few things that constituted "sin." I didn't think of myself as a "sinner" however, and didn't feel any particular need for forgiveness except every once in a while. When something really bothered my conscience, I wanted forgiveness but didn't know how to get it. And whenever I allowed myself to think about my fate following death, my thoughts would go something like this: "Well, from reading the Bible a little, I gather that God is, after all, a merciful God. I haven't really done too much that is actually bad. I guess everything will be all right."

Thanks be to God for rescuing me from that kind of ignorance!

Don Shinnick, a teammate, is a Christian. Over a period of time, he led me to an awareness of Christ. Finally, one night, on Don's urging, I prayed and verbally accepted Christ as my Saviour. I told God that I wanted to repent of my sins. I asked His forgiveness in Jesus' name. I told Him that I wanted to put all my faith and trust in Christ as my Saviour. I also told Him that I didn't understand this and asked that He send His Spirit to help me. True to His promise in Luke 11:13, He did.

From then on, I prayed daily. I John 1:9 (rsv) says, "If we confess our sins, he is faithful and just, and will forgive our sins and cleanse us from all unrighteousness."

The Holy Spirit's presence in my life made me more and more aware of my sins, at the same time pointing out the necessity of Christ, who paid for my sins on the cross.

Whereas before I had to force myself to read the Bible, now I could hardly put it down. Passages that had no meaning before now were full of meaning. From reading the Old Testament, I saw that the coming of Jesus had been promised by God for many years and that He was truly the promised Messiah. Those Scriptures beyond my understanding I simply prayed about. I believe God helps each believer to understand in due time (John 14:26; 16:13).

I began to understand that Christ saves us from the eternal punishment our sin has earned for us (John 3:16). But when I thought about eternal life, I just couldn't believe it applied to me. As I became acquainted with more and more Christians who *were* sure of eternal life, I knew my faith was falling short. I felt unworthy.

Then I came to realize that I would *always* be unworthy, but that my salvation had nothing to do with personal "worth." It was a gift. I came to see that if I really trusted and believed in Christ as my Saviour, He *would* save me and I could count it a *fact!*

"For by grace you have been saved through faith; and this is not your own doing, it is the gift of God—not because of works, lest any man should boast" (Ephesians 2:8,9, rsv).

As I grasped this truth, the Lord granted me the assurance of my salvation.

I believe in Jesus Christ as my all-sufficient Saviour, that through faith in Him my sins are forgiven and life everlasting has been given me. I know that some day I will "ever be with the Lord" (I Thessalonians 4:17). I know too that this is because of nothing I have done, but simply because of the grace of God in sending Christ.

God wants all of us to have this full assurance, for the Holy Spirit speaks through the Apostle John in I John 5:13 (RSV) saying,

"I write this to you who believe in the name of the Son of God, that you may *know* that you have eternal life."

Prayer

Dear merciful and loving Father, thank You for sending Your Son Jesus so that we might have the free gift of salvation through faith in Him. Like the Apostle Paul we ask that we may be strengthened through Your Spirit in the inner man, and that Christ may dwell in our hearts through faith. Help us to follow in Jesus' footsteps in daily life. We ask it in His name. Amen.

BILL WADE

Quarterback for Christ

Therefore if any man be in Christ, he is a new creature:
old things are passed away; behold, all things are become
new. II CORINTHIANS 5:17

WHEN SPORTS WRITERS and others ask me for my greatest thrill, they no doubt have in mind some dramatic
game or specific play that occurred during my collegiate
years at Vanderbilt University, my seven years with the
Los Angeles Rams, or my experience with the Chicago
Bears. They are usually surprised at my reply.

First of all, my most thrilling moment in football is
yet to come. In the game of life, however, my most thrilling moment to date would have to be the decision I
made after Navy officer Jim Wilson talked to me for
about six hours back in 1953. Though I had been
brought up in a Christian home, with wonderfully de-
vout parents, Jim impressed upon me the necessity for
a personal surrender to Jesus Christ as Saviour and
Lord. A new aim and purpose in my life resulted from
my spiritual transaction at that time.

In the game of pro football, there are many injuries
which could be avoided. The best way to escape these
is to keep your body physically fit.

When we consider life, whether it be for ten years or
a hundred, we are participating in a series of games.
We will readily admit that the game of life is basically

spiritual. As we play the game and learn our purpose, whether it be president of a bank, worker in a factory, secretary, or quarterback of a football team, we must exercise ourselves spiritually to win the daily battles.

I have found there are three basic exercises which strengthen me spiritually. The first is the exercise of prayer. The second is that of reading the Bible. The third is one that is vital to every Christian—that of asking in prayer each day that you might be allowed to talk to someone about the Christian way of life.

If you believe that God has created you, it becomes a supplemental belief that He has created you for a purpose. What purpose? This is answered when we submit ourselves to Him, that His will be done in our lives.

In talking to youth groups on the subject of "What It Takes To Play Football," I like this acrostic:

C—Confidence. ". . . If God be for us, who can be against us?" (Romans 8:31).

H—Humility. ". . . he that humbleth himself shall be exalted" (Luke 14:11).

R—Respect. We must have a respect for laws, of doing what is right. A healthy respect for others is vital to a fruitful Christian life.

I—Intelligence. As a quarterback, one must learn and know a great many things. To be good, useful Christians, we should be as intelligent as possible.

S—Sincerity. You must be sincere before people will believe you.

T—Truth. "Unto thine own self be true." Don't lie to yourself. Don't try to fool yourself by fooling others.

We can belong to Christ by opening our hearts, allowing Him to cleanse us from our sin, and personally accepting Him as Saviour and Lord of our life.

Prayer Suggestion

Open up all the way to Jesus Christ. Let Him guide you into a wonderful new life.

II

TRAINING

Spiritual Discipline

PAUL DIETZEL

Jesus the Man

I beseech you therefore, brethren, by the mercies of God,
that ye present your bodies a living sacrifice, holy, acceptable unto God, which is your reasonable service. And be
not conformed to this world: but be ye transformed by
the renewing of your mind, that ye may prove what is that
good, and acceptable, and perfect, will of God. ROMANS
12:1-2

WE HAVE HAD enough of the emaciated Christ, the pale,
anemic, namby-pamby Jesus.

Jesus of Nazareth was no physical weakling. He
couldn't have been and lived the life recorded in the
Gospels. Most of His earthly life He was a carpenter,
working with His hands in the days before power tools.

Consider too that everywhere Jesus went, He *walked*.
He walked up mountains, over deserts and beside the
sea. He walked from the northernmost point in Palestine
to the Holy City itself. Most athletes know there's no
exercise on earth that does more for over-all conditioning.

In spite of some artists' conceptions of Jesus, I do
not believe He was feeble and feminine in appearance.
Nobody like that could have walked through a "lynch-
ing mob" without a hand touching him or thrown over

the tables of the money-changers in the temple without suffering immediate reprisal.

When He was finally captured by His enemies, He was kept up all night undergoing questioning. Then He was tortured by the Romans. A crown of thorns was pressed down over His head. He was made to carry His own cross to the place of execution. Although He staggered under the weight of the burden and was aided, He endured without a murmur the driving of spikes into His hands and feet. And He hung for six hours in awful agony without a whimper. His first words from the cross were, "Father, forgive them; for they know not what they do."

I submit that Jesus of Nazareth was a strong, healthy, manly-appearing person whose body was firm muscled by honest toil and rigorous discipline. And I believe He expects each one of His followers to live healthy, disciplined lives to the limits of individual capability.

A Bible verse that is much misunderstood is Matthew 5:5: "Blessed are the meek: for they shall inherit the earth." Although we have come to think of another meaning for the word "meek," it is actually derived from the Greek word which means "harnessed, well-trained, disciplined."

We don't have to be athletes to live like this. The frailest body is a marvelous creation composed of countless thousands of joints and organs acting and interacting to sustain life. And this whole complex miracle, the body, is controlled by the mind.

Or should be.

Unfortunately, today there is a kind of conduct finding acceptance among young people that is labeled "modern." To "live modern," young people are urged to smoke, drink and abuse their bodies promiscuously.

The only "reason" advanced for this type of conduct is that others are doing the same things. Sometimes "big names" in the athletic world are paid to endorse cigarettes, tobacco and other products in order to add impetus to this "me-too" movement. Promoters of these "modern" habits hint that people who do not indulge themselves are "blue noses," "squares" and "sissies."

And, of course, they are dead wrong.

As Christians, we can set them straight as we live "harnessed, well-trained, disciplined" lives for Christ. Only then will the obvious benefits of the Christian life appear.

All of us—athletes or not—can live like this. It means nonconformance to the "world." It means a transformation of the mind. And it leads each of us to the discovery of "that good, and acceptable, and perfect, will of God."

To the society in which we live, it soon appears that what we are actually doing is "presenting our bodies" to God, keeping in top shape for His service. In this way, every Christian's life becomes an advertisement for Christ.

Determine today to live the vigorous, disciplined life of a real disciple.

Prayer

Heavenly Father, we thank Thee for the example of courage and discipline set for us by Thy Son, Jesus. We are unable to live like that in our own strength. But we believe that as we surrender our wills to Thee, we may be empowered to lead humble, trained, disciplined lives, "harnessed" to Thy purposes and subject to Thy pleasure. We ask that it may be so in Jesus' name. Amen.

OTTO GRAHAM

A Disciplined Faith

Do you remember how, on a racing-track, every competitor runs, but only one wins the prize? Well, you ought to run with your minds fixed on winning the prize! Every competitor in athletic events goes into serious training. Athletes will take tremendous pains—for a fading crown of leaves. But our contest is for an eternal crown that will never fade.

I run the race then with determination. I am no shadow-boxer, I really fight! I am my body's sternest master, for fear that when I have preached to others I should myself be disqualified. I CORINTHIANS 9:24-27 (PHILLIPS)

A DOZEN OR MORE recent tests have come to the same conclusion: America is physically unfit. More and more boys and girls are turning up in our schools with poor posture, flabby muscles and a lack of endurance. By contrast, the youth of Russia seem to be trained, hardened by athletics and disciplined, army style.

Part of our trouble in this country can be traced to the popular philosophy of "let's take it easy." With this attitude going the rounds, we shouldn't be surprised at the low level of national fitness. Because the boy or girl who wants a strong, healthy body must be willing to pay the price.

I applied this easy-going philosophy just once during

my ten years of professional football. It was 1955. I'd retired from active playing but agreed to rejoin the Cleveland Browns late in the exhibition schedule when they had lost the services of one of their two quarterbacks. I only had two weeks' practice before our first league game with the Washington Redskins.

Normally I start early in the week building up psychologically and physically for a football contest. Not just the night before the game, but two nights before are early-to-bed nights for me. While some players are packing away steaks on the day of the game, I limit myself to a chocolate bar. I always feel butterflies in my stomach.

But this time I decided to skip all that. For once I would enjoy a game. In the nights before the contest I went to bed when I felt like it. On the day of the game I had a wonderful steak. My stomach felt fine.

That day the Redskins clobbered us and I never played a sorrier game. The sports writers were kind in their write-ups saying, "Graham isn't in shape yet," but I knew the bitter truth: I'd tried to win while "taking it easy."

I believe America is also *spiritually* unfit for the challenges immediately ahead. And the reason is exactly the same. We're "taking it easy." Many people today tend to see Christianity as an "armchair" religion and God as an indulgent old gentleman with a fat purse. Actually, the God of the Bible is a God of justice with a keen sense of right and wrong.

Many schools are condemning basketball players for accepting outside money, while their so-called "scholarship systems" are the very essence of bribery. Huge corporations penalize their workers for misuse of company time, while on a high level, prices are "fixed" to cheat the government.

We are dead wrong if we think God is going to overlook this kind of injustice and hypocrisy. America must return to God. Only disciplined faith will be able to survive the kind of tests that face us in the future.

I experienced a faint shadow of the power of faith like this when I began to play professional football. It was a thrilling thing, realizing that my teammates trusted me. They were not always in a position to understand how I would direct the play as quarterback and I must admit that there were many times I was only guessing. But they disciplined themselves on the playing field into unquestioning obedience. They were convinced that I would always act in their best interests.

That's the secret of a strong faith. And I learned it more completely in 1952. In that year a baby was born in our family. My son lived just six weeks. And when it was over, there were moments of despair. If there were a God, why did He permit this? I have never received an answer to that question. But I have received a faith that can go on *without* the answer. That faith is the steady confidence that God will always have a reason for whatever happens.

Many people today have no conception of faith. They are completely absorbed in making money and "getting ahead." Their business is their life. But I believe your life is your business. And with real spiritual discipline, you should be bringing your interests, attitudes and desires into conformity with God's will each day.

I believe America is physically and spiritually unfit. But you can start today to change the picture by the measure of one life—your own. Leave to the crowd the philosophy of "let's take it easy." Line up with Jesus Christ who said, "If any man will come after me, let him deny himself, and take up his cross . . ." (Matthew 16:24).

Prayer

Heavenly Father, help me to discipline my body so that I may be physically fit. But more important, give me a trained and disciplined spiritual life. Strengthen my faith. I ask it in Jesus' name. Amen.

RAFER JOHNSON

Training To Win

> But whatever gain I had, I counted as loss for the sake of Christ. Indeed I count everything as loss because of the surpassing worth of knowing Christ Jesus my Lord. For his sake I have suffered the loss of all things, and count them as refuse, in order that I may gain Christ and be found in him, not having a righteousness of my own, based on law, but that which is through faith in Christ, the righteousness from God that depends on faith. PHILIPPIANS 3:7-9 (RSV)

IT IS SOMETIMES said that winning is not important, that the important thing is competing. But when we have to go to a hospital for an operation, we expect more from the surgeon than a "good try." We expect him to "win."

The same thing is true in sports. If the athlete thinks he will lose, he has lost already. Mental training is just as important as physical training. A record is broken because someone thinks he can do it. Although the real athlete doesn't always take first place, he is in each event with one determination: to win.

I believe Ty Cobb is a good example of this. In one game in which he came up to bat, he was walked. But on first base, he watched his chances and stole second. Then he stole third. Finally he stole home to score.

This is the type of athlete I'd like to have on any team I belong to.

Ducky Drake, my coach at U.C.L.A., said once, "When an athlete goes in for the decathlon seriously, it's not just a matter of physical conditioning and training—it's a whole way of life."

I found this to be true. I started training for the 1960 Olympics right after the 1956 Olympics. By the time I was through working out each day in preparation for the ten events of the decathlon, there wasn't much time left over for anything else. And these four years of preparation were not thought of simply as years leading up to good competition. I was determined to win.

But during the many years in which I have been training for athletic events, I have come to realize the greater importance of winning another kind of victory—victory in life. And I have come to realize too that I could never win this contest in my own strength.

I've attended church ever since I can remember. I can thank my mother and father for this, because they saw to it that their children attended Sunday school and church regularly. I was in the church choir, gave my offerings, and was, in general, very active in its program. But even with all my church activities, I was not sure that my life was lined up with God's will.

On October 29, 1953, I realized that I could never be lined up with His will until I accepted His Son Jesus Christ by faith as my personal Saviour. There wasn't much emotion as I did this but later, when I realized that He was blessing my commitment in many ways, the tears really flowed. I don't know when I've ever felt happier. Since then I have come to see how anyone can achieve victory in life through Jesus Christ. We experience this when we acknowledge that the achievement is all His. Through our faith, we share in His victory.

Depending upon Him this way, I found that I could face problems without fear and discouragement. No matter how big or small the problem, He was always present and ready to help. Philippians 4:13 is certainly true: "I can do all things in him who strengthens me" (RSV).

Without His help I could not participate in athletics. For He gave me an athletic body, good health and coordination, all so necessary in sports. And in the ten contests that make up the Olympic decathlon—running, jumping, throwing, for two long days—I know I couldn't have succeeded without His strength.

I come to each athletic event conditioned physically and mentally. But spiritual conditioning is the most important of all. This means I am prepared to run each race, compete in each contest, not for my glory but for the glory of my Lord.

Ever since I became a Christian in my junior year in high school, I have loved Jesus Christ with all my heart. He is the leader of my life and without Him I would be lost for He is all.

During high school I had the pleasure of playing on many championship teams. In college I had the same pleasure. During my years at U.C.L.A. I have had the privilege of running on track teams that have won the Pacific Coast Championship. Then, of course, the high privilege of representing my country in the 1956 and 1960 Olympic Games.

But as thrilling as it has been to belong to these great teams, I am more thrilled to be on the greatest team of all, the Christian team. Championships will soon be forgotten. Trophies grow tarnished and old. But the

Christian team will go on to greater and greater victories in Christ.

Prayer

Dear Lord, I thank You for every talent and every gift of life that You have given me. Help me to use these talents to the fullest. Help me to be physically and mentally prepared to do my best. Finally, help me to realize that the greatest victory—victory in life—can be won only in the strength of Your Son Jesus Christ. Grant that I may accept Him, love Him and follow Him all my days. I ask it in His name. Amen.

C. L. "Biggie" MUNN

Prayer

> And he said unto them, When ye pray, say, Our Father which art in heaven, Hallowed be thy name. Thy kingdom come. Thy will be done, as in heaven, so in earth. Give us day by day our daily bread. And forgive us our sins; for we also forgive every one that is indebted to us. And lead us not into temptation; but deliver us from evil. LUKE 11:2-4

As a youngster I was a restless kid with a lot of surplus energy. If there was a scrap somewhere, it was a fair bet that I was involved in some way. Once I was kicked out of school for a breach of conduct.

I lost my father when I was eight. My mother worked, and the whole family had to pull hard to keep going. I guess a lot of my aggressiveness sprang from the rough, uphill struggle to make a living that we all knew firsthand.

One day, a fellow named Clarence Angel appeared at our Junior High School. The name intrigued me and I liked the man's looks. In later months and years we became very fond of him. When he called his first meeting for boys at our school, I went along out of curiosity. A club was formed and everybody tried to think of a good name for it. Clarence told us about a missionary named Dr. Wilfred Grenfell, who spent most of his life in Labrador. A vote was taken and we became the Grenfell Club. When most of us moved into high school the following year, the club continued. Under the Christian leadership of Clarence Angel, it became clear to me that there was a God in heaven supervising the universe, a God who was the real source of all power.

One summer it was decided that the club would spend a couple of weeks camping together. Eager for the excitement of living for a time in the wilds, I went along too. After the day's fun on the trail, there was a roaring campfire and each boy bowed his head and prayed. As the silence of the wilderness was broken only by the crackling fire and the distant hooting of an owl, I sensed that I was communicating with that great God who kept the stars in their places. I began to believe that He could help me keep my life in place as well.

As the years rolled by, prayer came to mean more and more to me. When I entered coaching, I found my new tasks and duties were often a lonely business. There were burdens and concerns about the teams that couldn't be shared with the players or with anyone else. But in prayer I could face these problems with God.

I urged all my teams to consider prayer as a practice as important as the actual playing of the game. When I was head coach at Michigan State University, my football teams developed the habit of praying before every game. Not a prayer to win, but the simple recognition that the strength to play the game originates with God. It is always an experience to be with these young men as they kneel all around the locker room to recognize God in the moments preceding a game.

In 1951 we played Ohio State at Columbus and won the game in the last few seconds. It was a thrilling victory and surely a time when my boys could be excused for exuberant celebration. But moments after the final whistle, a young linebacker on our team, his face smeared with dirt and still breathing hard, came up to me and said, "Coach, if it was good to say a prayer before the game, why don't we say one afterward?" From that time on, our teams have met for prayer after every game as well as before—whether we won or lost.

I'd be the last to say that prayer can be used as a "technique" for securing victories. It goes a lot deeper than that. Prayer helps to develop men—men who recognize a supreme power in life far beyond themselves. But it seems a fact that when real men are being created, hard-fought games and victories always seem to follow as inevitable by-products.

Prayer produces unity everywhere. It is not only the "glue" that can hold a football team together; it is the "glue" that holds the Christian "team" together in its world-wide fellowship. The boy or girl who has no time for prayer is a loner. And there's no such thing as a loner in football or in Christianity. You either belong to the team or you don't.

So many people wait until they want something or until tragedy strikes them down before turning to prayer. But why shouldn't prayer be just as vital an experience in times of success? Jesus prayed when He was happy. He prayed when He felt sad.

If we will follow His example and make prayer an integral part of *all* our lives—before the game, after the game, and in the midst of the game—we will come to know the full meaning of fellowship with God.

Prayer

Dear Lord, forgive us in our failures and keep us humble in our successes. And teach us to pray in every circumstance of life. We ask it in Jesus' name. Amen.

CLENDON THOMAS

Bible Reading

Study to shew thyself approved unto God, a workman that needeth not to be ashamed, rightly dividing the word of truth. II TIMOTHY 2:15

And these words, which I command thee this day, shall be in thine heart: And thou shalt teach them diligently unto thy children, and shalt talk of them when thou sittest in thine house, and when thou walkest by the way, and when thou liest down, and when thou risest up. And thou shalt bind them for a sign upon thine hand, and they shall be as frontlets between thine eyes. And thou shalt write them upon the posts of thy house, and on thy gates. DEUTERONOMY 6:6-9

No REAL ATHLETE will agree to enter a game without first becoming familiar with the rule book. How are points scored? What is considered a foul? How many "time-outs" are allowed? What is the time limit on each game?

The Bible is the Christian's "rule book." In it he discovers the "rules of life." He learns what sin is. He learns what God in Christ has done about it. He learns how to respond in faith to God and how to live out that faith in daily life.

Students often excuse themselves from regular Bible study by pointing to their increasing load of homework.

But of what value is the accumulation of many kinds of knowledge if the one Book is neglected that gives knowledge its real meaning and purpose?

My own "rule book" is filled with underlined passages and the edges of its pages are crowded with notations. To me, it's a book of practical strategy in my day-by-day struggle against the forces of Satan. It's a "working book"—actually a "weapon." In fact, in Ephesians 6:17, the word of God is likened to a sword.

The Bible is an intensely personal book. I don't expect anybody else on earth to understand the notes I've written in mine. The Bible answers my current problems when I read it. And a year later I can come back to the same familiar passage and find new meanings there, meanings that help me with new problems being faced.

Of course the Bible doesn't speak to the condition of men by itself. Its truth is mediated. Its insights are granted only to those who have bound themselves in loyalty and devotion to the Book's Author. In a similar way, an athlete's rule book does him little good until he has signed on to play under the direction of a coach.

The Christian's coach is Christ. Commitment to Christ makes the Bible *your* book, initiates you into its wisdom and enables you to put this wisdom into practice.

And that's the important thing to remember about the Bible. Its truth was written to be put into practice.

Someone once described a football team this way: a center, two guards, two tackles, two ends, two halfbacks, a fullback and 50,000 quarterbacks in the grandstands."

It doesn't do much good to analyze correctly the opposing team's defense if you're sitting in the stands. And the insights gained through Bible reading are useless until we put them into action in daily life.

One of my favorite Bible personalities is Daniel. My

decision not to drink or smoke can be traced in part to my study of this Scriptural character. Daniel found himself in the midst of an alien and godless society. In spite of constant temptation, he kept himself spiritually disciplined and in good physical condition.

As we apply Scriptural truth to our own lives according to our leading, we become salesmen for Christ. We become, in fact, the only "Bibles" many people will ever read!

Ask yourself these three questions: Am I really looking to Christ as the "coach" of my life? Do I consider the Bible as the indispensable "rule book" for living? Do I seek its wisdom, guidance and encouragement daily?

Prayer Suggestion

In your own words, ask God to open to you the rich treasures of the Scriptures. Ask Him to deepen your affection for this Book and make Bible reading a daily habit. Ask Him for the grace to put some truth of the Bible into action in your life today.

ROE JOHNSTON

Reconciliation

All this is from God, who through Christ reconciled us to himself and gave us the ministry of reconciliation; that is, God was in Christ reconciling the world to himself, not counting their trespasses against them, and entrusting to us the message of reconciliation. So we are ambassadors for Christ, God making his appeal through us. We beseech you on behalf of Christ, be reconciled to God. II CORINTHIANS 5:18-20 (RSV)

WHEN I CAME out of the naval service in 1946, I wanted to go into industrial relations. I'd done much studying and thinking about this important field and I felt I could help to work out some of the differences that existed between labor and management.

But in the months that followed, I experienced a rude awakening. Although there was a certain amount of success achieved at the conference table, I was dismayed by another phenomenon. Time after time I saw a constructive suggestion taken as a threat, a concession treated as ground gained on a battlefield, and a few minor difficulties magnified by suspicion into first-class problems.

I finally left industry and entered the service of the church. I had become convinced that men will never be really reconciled with each other until they are first reconciled to God. In the years that have followed, I have seen dramatic examples of how this works.

The church I serve in Indianapolis is located in an area of the city that is a conflux of a dozen cultural and economic groups. For this reason, misunderstanding, suspicion and tension are part of the air we breathe.

In our own church, for example, two youth groups met, which were completely different in social and economic backgrounds. One was made up of the youngsters in our old-line families that had moved to the suburbs but continued active in the church; the other was made up of kids in the immediate neighborhood who lived in near-slumlike conditions.

These two groups met at different times and did not mingle. Between them there existed the usual stereotyped attitudes and suspicions.

But one day in one of the meetings someone suggested that the two groups come together for a joint meeting.

It was quite a sight—the ivy-league suits and conservative dresses on one side of the room. And on the other, girls in sweater and skirt combinations and boys in black jackets. But after the atmosphere had thawed, there was discussion, frank exchange of opinion and worship. And each group found that members of the other group were not such "squares" after all.

Out of that meeting and others that followed, there developed a Teen Council to plan programs to interest other teenagers in the neighborhood. A Teen Canteen was started with "Open House" in the church basement every Friday and Saturday night. A dozen activities were offered and a snack bar stocked with light refreshments.

Our neighborhood is a tough neighborhood and in

the beginning it was almost necessary to "frisk" the "hoods" that drifted in with their girls, in order to stop the surreptitious drinking. Once there was a full-scale rumble on the front lawn of the church that had to be broken up by the police.

But, little by little, those who had become reconciled to God and then to each other began to spread the contagion of their reconciliation to the wider circle beyond. "What's the church doing this for?" boys and girls, who had known nothing like healthy recreation or Christian concern, began to ask.

When a nearby place of business practically sponsored teen-age prostitution, the Teen Council at the church went into action. Together with officers of the juvenile aid division of the police department, this "organized immorality" was brought to a stop. A point of interest: many members of the Teen Council who fought this evil had police records themselves, going back to the years before the church reached them.

What happened was this: they had become reconciled to God. Reconciliation means to be "won back." All of us have come from God and we are exiles until somehow we get back to Him.

The task of winning us back was taken on by Jesus Christ. This was the reason He came. This was the point of His teaching. This is the deepest meaning of His cross.

As we freely accept from Him the forgiveness and new life He offers, we find that we are back with God. As one teen-ager said about the Teen Canteen after a long absence, "This feels like coming home."

We "come home" to God through faith in Jesus Christ. Then an amazing thing happens. We find that we have been entrusted with the "message of reconciliation" and must pass it on to others. There is no sense of superiority in this. Basically, Christianity is one hungry man telling another hungry man how to find bread, with this difference: the "bread" of reconciliation multiplies as we share it. And it completely satisfies.

Prayer

Gracious Father in Heaven, we thank Thee for Thy Son Jesus Christ who brings us out of darkness into the light of Thy presence. Help us to pass on the precious message of reconciliation that others also may know peace of heart and "come home" to Thee. We ask it in Jesus' name. Amen.

VERNON LAW

Witnessing

> Ye are the light of the world. A city that is set on an hill cannot be hid. Neither do men light a candle, and put it under a bushel, but on a candlestick; and it giveth light unto all that are in the house. Let your light so shine before men, that they may see your good works, and glorify your Father which is in heaven. MATTHEW 5:14-16

THE STORY IS told of a sixteenth-century duke who had ten daughters he loved dearly. As the years sped by, he decided to leave them something to remember him by and constructed a beautiful chapel.

At last came the great day when the work was finished and the duke took his daughters to see it. The simple lines, the graceful beams, the magnificent carvings and the glowing stained-glass windows took their breath away.

"But father," one daughter said suddenly, "where are the lamps?"

"That, my dear, is a special feature of the chapel," said the duke. "There will be no hanging lamps. Each person coming here to worship will carry his own lamp. I have provided small bronze lamps, one for every person in the village, up to the number the church will hold."

Then he added slowly, "Some corner of God's House

63

will be dark and lonely, if all His sons and daughters do not come to worship Him at the appointed time."

Four hundred years have passed since that time and the bronze lamps have been handed down from father to son and carefully treasured. When the sweet-toned bells of the old church ring today, the village people wend their way up the hill, each carrying his own lamp. The church is nearly always filled, for no family wishes its corner to be dark.

This story by Elizabeth Cheney expresses just the way I feel about witnessing. Jesus said His followers were "lights" and He commanded them to let that light "shine." When any Christian fails to share his faith with others, his particular corner of the kingdom stays dark and gloomy.

Much of the world today is dark. Part of the reason is that Christians have been too careful not to offend the forces of darkness. They have come to believe that conforming to the world will put us in a better position to influence it for good. They have forgotten that the value of light lies not in its similarity to darkness but in its glaring contrast.

Other people are continually asking, "Can I smoke or drink and still be a Christian?" This kind of question betrays a fundamentally wrong attitude. The true Christian is not trying to discover how many doubtful activities he can engage in and still be considered a member of the brotherhood. He is too busy trying to find out how he can more effectively impress the society around him with the claims of his Master.

It is hard to say who is blessed most when a Christian shares his faith: the Christian, or the person receiving the good news of the gospel. Witnessing exercises every spiritual faculty of the believer. He must spend time with his Bible, wait for God's direction, pray in faith, and go out rejoicing.

Witnessing is hard only when we try to do it all by ourselves. If we have a certain amount of eloquence, it is a temptation to believe we can "talk" someone into discipleship. Sometimes men of learning are tempted to believe they can "teach" people into the kingdom. But the human soul is not moved in its deepest parts by clever arguments or great knowledge. Men and women become disciples only when they have been inwardly transformed by the Holy Spirit.

For this reason, witnessing is not something to be rushed into. There is a time to speak and a time to be silent. There are people to speak to and others who are not your spiritual responsibility. And the Christian who waits for orders before acting will find that eloquence and great knowledge are not needed—just humility and an obedient spirit.

Another story is told about a passenger on an ocean liner who was lying in his stateroom, deathly sick. Suddenly the cry was heard, "Man overboard!" The ill passenger struggled to his feet but he was so weak he could barely stand. All he could manage to do was grab his flashlight and shine it out his porthole.

The drowning man was saved. Later he said, "I was going down for the last time when someone put a light in a porthole. It shone on my hand. A sailor in a lifeboat saw me and pulled me in."

Was it a small thing, the shining of the flashlight from the porthole? It didn't require a profound knowledge of seamanship. It didn't require cleverness. It didn't even require that the passenger be in the pink of good health. But it saved a man's life.

This is true of witnessing. One kind word spoken at

the right time to the right person can result in a changed life.

No disciple is exempt. Each one carries his own lamp. Will you carry yours today?

Prayer

Lord, I pray that this day my light may so shine before those I meet that they may feel the impulse to glorify Thee. I ask it in Jesus' name. Amen.

DAVE FERRIS

The Inner Conversation

Be careful for nothing; but in every thing by prayer and
supplication with thanksgiving let your requests be made
known unto God. And the peace of God, which passeth all
understanding, shall keep your hearts and minds through
Christ Jesus. PHILIPPIANS 4:6

I TALK TO God about everything. I can be driving a car
or walking or sitting around with friends enjoying a
conversation. It doesn't matter. He's always present.
And I can turn to Him instantly with any question, any
problem, any small joy or sorrow.

Of course I've turned to Him in some pretty exciting
and challenging moments too.

I'd just gotten out of the service in April of 1945
when I was called up by the Red Sox from their Louisville farm club. I had seen only two major league ball
games when I found a baseball in my locker one day.
The Red Sox have a way of notifying a rookie pitcher
who is to work his first game. No one says anything to
him. He just finds a baseball in his locker.

When I saw this baseball lying there in my locker
for the first time, I began to feel weak in the knees.
The other players changed into their uniforms and
trotted outside to warm up, but I stayed behind in the
locker room. I prayed for strength and courage. I

prayed that God would permit me to play the best game I was capable of.

Later, on the mound, looking down the line at the first batter, I was still shaky but beginning to feel that God was going to take care of things. I was pitching against Bobo Newsom of the Philadelphia Athletics in front of 30,000 people. I'd never seen that many people together in one place in all my life.

Out of my first fifteen throws to the plate, fourteen were balls. Only God knows why I wasn't pulled out of the game right then. The bases were loaded. And the count mounted to 3 and 2 as Dick Seibert faced me at the plate. The only pitch that wasn't a ball had been popped up. So there was one out.

Strange to say, during all of this, I was growing more quiet inside, more certain that God would not fail me.

Then suddenly there was a grounder to short. Skeeter Newsome grabbed it, stepped on second and threw to first for a double play. The threat was over.

I went on in that game to pitch a shut-out.

Sometimes you don't win though. In the World Series of 1946 against the Cardinals, I prayed again that I'd be permitted to do my best. I pitched a 4-0 shut-out in the third game. But we went on to lose the series 4-3.

In 1949 I prayed for strength without much apparent success. That was the year I injured my shoulder. Nothing can be a greater disaster for a pitcher. It looked as though I was finished with baseball. I just couldn't make the ball go where I wanted it to. I grew more and more discouraged.

Little by little though, I began to see that God had other gifts to give besides strength and courage. In 1950 I was back in the minors playing in Birmingham and Louisville. But I was discovering that God still owned the universe.

It was at Louisville that I was first given the opportunity to coach and a few years later I was moved back to the Red Sox as a full-fledged pitching coach. I'd learned the meaning of the verse, "And we know that all things work together for good to them that love God, to them who are the called according to his purpose" (Romans 8:28).

I learned too that God always answers even when we don't know exactly what to pray for. These "surprises" have led me to my present prayer habits. I don't try to figure out exactly what I want and then fire off a single petition. God isn't running a mail-order business where it's important to get each catalog number correct on the order blank.

Jesus is a friend of mine. And you can "let your hair down" with a friend. You can be yourself and admit you don't know what you'd like or what's best for you.

You can't rush friendship either. Just as God permits us time to find ourselves and respond to Him, He requires time to work out His will in our lives. Waiting upon God is just as important as prayer itself.

A few years ago the Presbyterian Church in the U.S. asked me if I would write a small pamphlet on the subject of tithing. I'm no writer. The prospect of putting together this tract filled me with more dread than facing a battery of major-league batting stars. So I prayed about it. I talked to God about my limitations in this area. And in the silent recesses of my heart, He talked back. Soon I became convinced that He wanted me to write the tract anyway.

I had several months to get the material together and

during the first few months, almost nothing occurred to me. Then, little by little, the thoughts began to come. After a night game in Kansas City, I got on a train for Chicago and settled back in my seat. Almost unbidden, thoughts on this subject began to flow through my mind, arranging themselves in an orderly fashion. I dug out my pencil and began to scribble. There was no effort. Three days later, it was all wrapped up.

I sent it to Presbyterian headquarters and according to their latest report the pamphlet, entitled "The Thrill of Tithing," is still being extensively used.

Prayer is conversation. The best prayer is spontaneous, unstilted and genuine. The important thing is the desire to keep in touch with God. It doesn't take a lot of knowledge or effort or a big vocabulary. It doesn't take a lot of preparation or a special time of day.

Start now. *Right now.* Don't think thoughts by yourself. Share them with God. Tell Him how you feel. Nothing is unimportant or uninteresting to Him. Don't worry about offending Him by not "saying it right." Look at Abraham and Job and Jacob and Jonah. They weren't perfect men. Some of their prayers were not exactly admirable. But there's one thing these men didn't do: they didn't stop praying. And so they were blessed.

You can be too!

Prayer

Dear Lord, teach me the habit of unceasing prayer. Grant me the joy that comes from knowing Thy companionship. Help me to turn to Thee quickly, spontaneously, as one friend to another. And grant that I may start enjoying this experience right now. I ask it in Jesus' name. Amen.

GIL DODDS

Patience

And he tarried seven days, according to the set time that
Samuel had appointed: but Samuel came not to Gilgal;
and the people were scattered from him. And Saul said,
Bring hither a burnt offering to me, and peace offerings.
And he offered the burnt offering. And it came to pass,
that as soon as he had made an end of offering the burnt
offering, behold, Samuel came; and Saul went out to meet
him, that he might salute him. And Samuel said, What
hast thou done? I SAMUEL 13:8-11

Wherefore seeing we also are compassed about with so
great a cloud of witnesses, let us lay aside every weight,
and the sin which doth so easily beset us, and let us run
with patience the race that is set before us. . . . HEBREWS
12:1

. . . the trying of your faith worketh patience. But let
patience have her perfect work, that ye may be perfect
and entire, wanting nothing. JAMES 1:3

PATIENCE IS one of the great secrets of success in track.
But it took me a long time to learn it.

When I was a sophomore at Ashland College, Ohio,
I was given my first opportunity to race in Madison
Square Garden. I was being coached by mail by an old
friend (Ashland had no track team) and he advised
caution. But I was so thrilled at the chance to run in
the famous arena that nothing could hold me down. I

promised myself I'd run the legs off every other man in the race.

But I lacked experience in the elbowing, shouldering crush of big indoor track races. And long before the grueling two miles were over, I was bumped and jostled, thrown off stride, and finally dumped from the track completely. I climbed back onto the boards again in a dazed condition and staggered for a hundred yards or more bouncing off one side of the runway and then the other. As if from a great distance, I heard the 18,000 people in the stands booing me.

Then the runners, who by this time had lapped me, were jostling into me again. And this time I was sent sprawling. In a towering rage, the track director marched up and ordered me out of Madison Square Garden. I was commanded never to show my face there again.

I went back to college much chastened and settled down to begin training again, determined to listen to my coach and forget about whipping the world. But in my senior year it happened again. In a meet held in Beloit, Wisconsin, I ran a 4:13-minute mile. The fever started to build in me once more.

After graduation, I was determined to enter big-time competition. I really wanted to run and I'd prayed about it. But I was impatient. I wrote everybody I could think of who might be interested in sponsoring an up-and-coming runner. And the result was exactly —nothing!

Chastened once more, I decided to wait on the Lord. If He wanted me to run, He would make a way. And if He didn't want me to run, nothing on earth I could do would make me a champion.

A short time later, I received a letter from Walter Brown with an offer to run for the Boston Athletic Association. He invited me to come East at his expense and offered to help me find a job while I trained.

It wasn't until later that I found out the chain of events that led to that letter. Following my graduation, my high school and college coach (the one who had coached me by mail at Ashland) wrote a letter to Jack Ryder at Boston College who had once coached *him*. In due time, Ryder contacted Walter Brown and Mr. Brown wrote me. It was clear that God was working things out for me to run but He was working things out on *His* schedule, not mine!

The months passed swiftly after that. I came East and began to train under Jack Ryder. Under his coaching my time dropped lower and lower for the mile and two mile. In the years between 1944-55, in God's own good time, He gave me opportunity after opportunity to run against the world's greatest track men in Madison Square Garden and elsewhere.

Patience seems to be the hardest virtue to practice in life as well as in track. All around us we can see Christians hustling and bustling in the service of the Lord. And one wonders if the Lord has even been consulted about half of the projects underway!

If many of us were really frank, we would confess to a suspicion that God is a bit sleepy and slow in carrying out His will. Perhaps this explains the popular notion that He looks like an old man with a long white beard! But how else can we explain the fact that so often when we are prepared to do something for God's kingdom and the "perfect" opportunity opens up, it seems that the heavens are strangely silent! Often we

THE GOAL AND THE GLORY

go ahead and do the "obviously good" thing, only to find out later with disappointment that we have missed out on the best!

This was Saul's experience. He had great physical attributes. He was a giant of a man. And he had leadership ability and humility too—in the beginning. But he lacked patience. Samuel told him to wait until his arrival so that the aged prophet of God might make the required sacrifices properly. But Samuel was late in coming. And as the time dragged on, Saul yielded to the pressures of the moment. He made the sacrifices himself "to expedite matters" and in the process, lost his kingdom, his reason and finally his soul.

It takes patience to be a good disciple of Jesus Christ. He was not impressed with the swaggering boasts made by Simon Peter and he will not be impressed with the great sacrifices and daring deeds that we may offer Him. He is looking instead for patient men and women who will quietly wait for His time, His plan, His empowerment and His glory. These are the only people He will use.

Are *you* available to Him?

Prayer

Our Heavenly Father, quiet all my eager strivings to do great things for Thee. Help me to see that nothing avails that is not initiated by Thee. Nothing prevails that is not directed by Thee. And nothing succeeds that is not carried to its conclusion by Thee. I ask it in Jesus' name. Amen.

ALVIN DARK

Stewardship

> And why take ye thought for raiment? Consider the lilies of the field, how they grow; they toil not, neither do they spin: And yet I say unto you, That even Solomon in all his glory was not arrayed like one of these. Wherefore, if God so clothe the grass of the field, which to day is, and to morrow is cast into the oven, shall he not much more clothe you, O ye of little faith? Therefore take no thought, saying, What shall we eat? or, What shall we drink? or, Wherewithal shall we be clothed? (For after all these things do the Gentiles seek:) for your heavenly Father knoweth that ye have need of all these things. But seek ye first the kingdom of God, and his righteousness; and all these things shall be added unto you. MATTHEW 6:28-33

DID YOU EVER hear that famous verse, "God helps those who help themselves"? It's one of the most popular verses quoted by modern man today. And it's usually brought up to make one point: trust God all you want, but when it comes to making a living, brother, you're on your own!

Actually this statement cannot be found in the Bible. It is foreign to the spirit and teaching of the Bible. Instead, Jesus taught that caring for man's physical needs is just as much God's business as caring for man's

75

spiritual needs. And if a man will trust Him, God will provide everything necessary.

If we are really Christians, we do not work just "to make a living." If we play ball or clerk in a bank or sell neckties, it is because He has chosen to provide for our needs that way—not because we'd starve to death if we didn't.

When the Braves traded me to the Giants in 1949, a cigarette company approached a number of players for testimonials. Five hundred dollars was paid for each player's quoted endorsement of the brand. But I explained that, as a Christian, I felt smoking and drinking were very harmful to most people and I didn't want to influence anybody to begin these two habits. Some of the boys couldn't understand how I could pass up $500 so easily.

But the next day, Leo Durocher called me into his office to tell me I'd been appointed captain of the Giants for that year. With the appointment went a sum of money—exactly $500.

We are tempted to feel that we are at the mercy of circumstances. But the fact of the matter is that we are *masters* of our circumstances when we put our faith in Christ. He has overcome the world and He invites us to share in His victory. ". . . we are more than conquerors through him that loved us" (Romans 9:37). "He that spared not his own Son, but delivered him up for us all, how shall he not with him also freely give us all things?" (Romans 8:32).

Because of these mighty promises, we Christians are freed from the tight-fisted, fearful miserliness of the world around us. We are sons of the One who owns the universe and every resource of earth and heaven can be released in our assistance if He chooses.

I've been particularly blessed in being brought up in a Christian home where tithing was a regular practice. Giving the first tenth of my income back to God was just as unquestioned as putting on my socks before my shoes. And a nickel out of every fifty cents was quite a lot when I got up every day before dawn to pedal around my paper route. But as the years went by and my income increased, I found out I could never win in this game of giving to God. He always outgave me. He gave to me physically, financially and in a dozen other ways. He led me into a satisfying career in baseball and selected a wonderful girl to be my wife. And He has given me even more—salvation in His Son, Jesus Christ, peace of heart, joy, and the hope of heaven.

I learned that tithing is just a symbol of my trust in Him. Actually, if I belong to Him, He owns me and my income too, all of it. Tithing is just a signpost that indicates the direction a man's soul is leaning.

"For where your treasure is, there will your heart be also" (Matthew 6:21).

Prayer

Lord Jesus, keep me today from the world's fearful concern for self-preservation. Help me to see that Thou hast promised to care for my every need. Grant me trust and joy as I commit my life to Thee. Amen.

WILMA RUDOLPH

Guidance

Gracious is the Lord, and righteous;
    our God is merciful.
The Lord preserves the simple;
    when I was brought low, he saved me.
Return, O my soul, to your rest;
    for the Lord has dealt bountifully with you.
For thou hast delivered my soul from death,
    my eyes from tears,
    my feet from stumbling. . . .
PSALM 116:5-8 (RSV)

I FOUND OUT comparatively early in life that it takes a lot of trying to get anything worthwhile accomplished.

When I was only fifteen, I went to Melbourne, Australia, to participate in the Olympics. It wasn't publicized at the time and it was just as well. I had been lazy in practice and in running too. I simply had not done my best. After the Melbourne meet, I had plenty of time to think about my attitude. I came to realize that you have to give your best if you want to win.

So when I went to Rome for the 1960 Olympics, I had already made that truth a part of my life. I had worked hard in preparation. I was in top condition and in the right frame of mind for the events to come.

During our time in Rome my coach and the members

of our team got together for prayer from time to time. We felt that with God's help and with each of us doing his best, we could win. In a situation like this, it is a real temptation to pray to win. But we all asked God only to help us do our best. I personally felt that I had let my coach and teammates down in Melbourne. Now I wanted to win and do my best for them.

I asked God for special guidance in the opening event, the 100 meters. I ran hard and won. Later I paused and thanked Him for His being with me. My teammates and I came away with a record number of gold medals. But without God's help and His will in my life, I might have repeated my failure at Melbourne.

I feel I owe God a great deal for what He has done in all of my life. When I was about a year old, I contracted polio. The doctors told my mother that I would never walk. For over three years I made trips to the hospital for treatment and mother would get the same discouraging prediction. But my mother had great faith. Her faith told her to work with me and that with God's help, something could be done.

She worked with me daily, never giving up hope that I could be as normal as any other child. She took me and my brothers and sisters to church every Sunday. Every night we had family devotions. She instilled in all of us the love of God and the importance of giving Him our lives. If it hadn't been for my mother's efforts, I would never have walked, much less competed in the Olympics.

I don't know right now just what my plans are for future events. But I am running and keeping in condition every day. I don't want to do anything less than my best when I try. That day in Melbourne taught me that.

I've learned something else too. A Christian athlete is not a person who practices Christianity only on the track or playing field. God goes with me wherever I go, whether to the Olympics or to class or a party. He guides all of my life, day by day. He is in charge of my future.

There is nothing as important as having God close to you to guide and direct. Win or lose, I want to do His will always.

Prayer

Heavenly Father, I thank Thee for Thy mercy and loving kindness. I thank Thee for hearing and answering prayer, for giving direction to our lives and for standing by patiently as we learn to know Thy love. In Jesus' name. Amen.

III

PLAYING THE GAME

Living for Christ

DONN MOOMAW

Jesus the Christ

Have this mind among yourselves, which you have in Christ Jesus, who, though he was in the form of God, did not count equality with God a thing to be grasped, but emptied himself, taking the form of a servant, being born in the likeness of men. And being found in human form he humbled himself and became obedient unto death, even death on a cross. Therefore God has highly exalted him and bestowed on him the name which is above every name, that at the name of Jesus every knee should bow, in heaven and on earth and under the earth, and every tongue confess that Jesus Christ is Lord, to the glory of God the Father. PHILIPPIANS 2:5-11 (RSV)

OFTEN WE FORGET that Jesus did not come into existence as a babe in Bethlehem. He left the royal garments of a king to don swaddling clothes. He stepped down from the battlements of heaven, where He commanded legions of angels, to become the child of a peasant girl.

Bethlehem does not erase the fact that Jesus has always been Lord of all history. We do not make Him Lord. He *is* Lord. The Bible speaks this central truth from Genesis to Revelation.

And if He is Lord, then He is alive.

With this truth before us, how can we groan with the changes of history? How can we become discouraged or despair when the headlines tell of the triumph of evil men?

The Lord of all creation lives! Think of it! If we fully realized this fact, we would never frown again. We couldn't keep from shouting for sheer joy. This was the fact that sent the first-century disciples out upon an amazed world after the resurrection of Jesus. They could scarcely contain themselves. They stammered. They stuttered. They tried to express the earth-shaking news and observers recorded tongues of fire standing on each man. Small wonder their enthusiasm on that first day captured 3000 converts!

And what was their message? *"He is alive!"*

What if the United Nations would believe this!

What if the Security Council and the heads of states and the men of authority in every land would believe this!

What if *you*—as you read this page—would believe it!

Because it's *true!* Jesus is just as powerful now as He was in the days of His flesh when He made the blind to see and the lame to walk and raised the dead to life again. And He stands ready to perform even greater marvels—to cause warring tribes to be at peace, to heal the nations and bring in His own Kingdom of justice and love.

Jesus Christ exercises His Lordship in three ways:

First, he is a *Prophet.* A prophet is one who declares, proclaims, reveals. And Jesus is still the only "revealer" of God. While most of humanity guesses about the divine identity and builds rival religions around its suppositions, Jesus says plainly. "He who hath seen me hath seen the Father"; "I am the Way, the Truth and the Life."

Our spiritual lives begin when we see God in the face of Jesus Christ.

On the final night of last summer's Fellowship of Christian Athletes' summer conference at Estes Park, Colorado, 750 of America's finest athletes stood with hands clasped, looking at a giant picture of Jesus as they sang "The Lord's Prayer" in a mighty chorus. I saw some of the roughest, toughest athletes you'd want to meet weeping unashamedly as they sang—weeping at the revelation of God they had received through Jesus Christ, the great Revealer.

Jesus is also *Priest*. With His coming, the old priestly rule described in such detail in the Old Testament is gone. It is no longer necessary for the high priest to go behind the veil of the temple into the holy of holies once a year to offer sacrifices.

Every time you and I cry out, "O God, be merciful to me, a sinner!" Christ, the great high priest, intercedes for us. And the one sacrifice He made on the cross two thousand years ago proves sufficient again and again and again. His healing, cleansing, forgiving office of priest is exercised every minute of every day in behalf of those who trust Him.

Finally, Jesus is *King*. And He said, "My kingdom is not of this world." We owe it to our ruler to live faithfully as subjects of His kingdom and not in thralldom to the times and seasons and material possessions that occupy the minds and hearts of those who pay no allegiance to Christ.

If He is our King, then He is King over everything— over our financial life, our domestic life, our social life, over affairs of the mind and the concerns of the heart. His sovereignty extends to the smallest decision we make.

Have *you* seen Jesus the Prophet and under His teaching, seen God the Father revealed? Have *you* seen Jesus the Priest and under His ministry found forgiveness and cleansing? Have *you* seen Jesus the King and made Him the undisputed monarch of all your life?

Prayer

Thou, O God, art all the world needs. Thou, O God, art all we need. Help us to find Thee as we recognize the mighty Lordship of Thy Son, Jesus Christ. We ask it in His name. Amen.

BUDDY DIAL

Desire

> So when they had dined, Jesus saith to Simon Peter, Simon, son of Jonas, lovest thou me more than these? He saith unto him, Yea, Lord; thou knowest that I love thee. He saith unto him, Feed my lambs.
>
> He saith to him again the second time, Simon, son of Jonas, lovest thou me? He saith unto him, Yea, Lord; thou knowest that I love thee. He saith unto him, Feed my sheep.
>
> He saith unto him the third time, Simon, son of Jonas, lovest thou me? Peter was grieved because he said unto him the third time, Lovest thou me? And he said unto him, Lord, thou knowest all things; thou knowest that I love thee. Jesus saith unto him, Feed my sheep. JOHN 21:15-17

I AM CONVINCED that desire is more important in an athlete than native ability.

Bobby Layne, the great all-American from the University of Texas, is an example of this. Doak Walker said, "Layne has never lost a game. Time just ran out on him."

Desire has meant a lot in my life too. In the little east Texas community where I grew up, I was smaller in size than most other boys my age. I was awkward too and lacked coordination. It was tough getting into the sand-lot games. The bigger, faster fellows were always chosen first. Time and again I was the only one left when both teams had been picked.

But I had a tremendous desire to be a football player. Everywhere I went I carried a football with me. I begged other boys to play catch. To develop "touch" in my hands and fingers, I used to lie on my back at night in my bedroom and throw the football in the air for hours. Catching it again and again in the darkness gradually taught my fingers to develop "eyes" of their own.

Desire is the most important element in Christianity too. My mother helped me to realize this. Many times during my boyhood she would say, "Christ gave His all for you, son. What are you going to give to Him?"

Then one night as my mother lay very sick of a serious disease, I sat at the kitchen table by myself and thought about this question again. What *had* I given to Christ? I had accepted Him as my Saviour but most of the decisions I made from day to day were my own. I had a desire to love and serve Him but it was a weak desire.

I don't want to be misunderstood. I was not "bargaining" with God. I was genuinely convinced of my spiritual lack and anxious to have something done about it. But the doctors had told me that the person I loved more than anyone else on earth was in serious condition. "Dear God," I prayed, "if You'll heal her, I'll live for You with all my heart."

The following day a medical examination revealed that every trace of the disease had disappeared from my mother's body. Today, years later, she is still alive and well.

And I kept my promise to God. I opened areas of my

life I'd been keeping closed. I started letting Him make all the decisions. And the result surprised me. A mighty desire to love and serve Christ took hold of me. And a great desire too that everybody else in the world might know Him.

Blessings and joys and wonders I'd thought fantastic before, now became a regular part of my life. Exhausted after a series of running plays, I've prayed silently and felt a surge of energy push through me as though a new dynamo had been cut in. In short, the presence of Christ is just as real to me on the playing field as in church. And why not? I belong to Him. I'm playing for Him. My football career was His idea long before I thought of it.

I believe we Christians limit ourselves. We decide just how much of our lives ought to be under God's direct command. And we decide too just how and when He can help us. As a result we miss the "abundant life" Jesus said He came to give us. We find we have little desire to love and serve Him.

The disciples limited themselves. They expected Jesus' kingdom to be an earthly one. So they committed only enough of themselves to accommodate their tiny concept of His ministry. They argued about who should be the greatest among them; they worried about the opposition of Rome, the weather at sea, how to feed the crowds who followed them. As a result they were totally unprepared for the challenge of the cross. Their desire to love and serve Jesus was not strong enough. They ran away and hid.

Only after the resurrection did some of them realize their lack. This is why Jesus cross-examined Peter and asked three times, "Do you love me?"

In other words, "How much do you love me? How great is your desire? How much does your faith in me mean?"

Are *you* short of desire? Perhaps it's because you haven't committed enough of yourself to Him.

Prayer

Dear Lord, You have given Your life for me on the cross. What have I given You? Help me to answer this question honestly. If a deeper commitment of my life is necessary, help me to make such a commitment right now. Above all, increase my desire to love and serve You. I ask it in Jesus' name. Amen.

DAN TOWLER

Acknowledging Him

Trust in the Lord with all thine heart; and lean not to thine own understanding. In all thy ways acknowledge him, and he shall direct thy paths. PROVERBS 3:5,6

. . . he that glorieth, let him glory in the Lord. II CORINTHIANS 10:17

YOU WILL EITHER acknowledge God in your life today or you will acknowledge yourself. There is no in-between. Either you will act as though God were a living Presence in all you do and say or you will act as though you were the Prime Mover yourself. And it will be apparent to everyone who observes you.

During three awful days in June of 1950, this truth was driven home to me with force.

That was the month I left my home town and traveled west to join the Los Angeles Rams at their training camp in California. There had been a number of favorable press notices surrounding my signing into professional football. And I'd committed the unpardonable sin of a professional athlete right at the beginning: I'd believed my own clippings.

As a result I came to the training camp with a sense of self-importance. I wasn't just another one of the rookies. I was a VIP. And I expected the other men to

91

recognize this. Not too surprisingly, I found other men there with *their* clippings. And *they* were waiting for recognition too. This produced some situations that seem amusing in retrospect, but which were not so funny at the time.

For instance, lights in the dormitories were supposed to be out at 11 o'clock each night. But I knew that crossing the room from my bunk to the light switch for this menial duty was certainly outside the dignity of *my* position. And since both of my roommates felt exactly the same way, the lights stayed on long after eleven, until the coach himself stopped by and turned them off.

In Redlands, California, in summer, the shades must be drawn during the heat of the day or the nights become insufferable. But once again, I felt that drawing those shades was a task beneath my dignity. And my roommates felt the same. As a result, we nearly suffocated with the heat for two nights.

On the third evening after dinner, I went to my room and locked the door. I opened my suitcase and took out the Bible that was packed away there (undisturbed since my arrival in camp).

At home and in college, I had read my Bible every evening and taken time to review each day with God. But somehow, in the long, 2000-mile trip to an unfamiliar part of the country, I'd come to feel that this was unnecessary. But now I knew I'd been wrong. It was clear to me that for three whole days, my life had drifted aimlessly.

I asked Christ to take over again. I turned over to Him all my new relationships: to my roommates, the coaches and others. I told him the anxieties I had about making the team, anxieties I'd been trying to hide from myself. I asked Him to give me the ability to get along with the other fellows and to be a real part of the team for as long as I played.

I opened the Bible and read Proverbs 3:6: "In all thy ways acknowledge him, and he shall direct thy paths." I knew now what had been the trouble. For three days I had been acknowledging myself and seeking acknowledgment from others. And for those same three days, I had failed to acknowledge *Him*.

When I arose from my knees, I had regained my sense of purpose. I knew why I was at training camp, why I was in professional football. I was there to glorify God with the talent He had given me.

As a young man, Dwight L. Moody had been a shoemaker. And about that early part of his life he said, "I drove nails in shoes for the glory of God."

I resolved to throw passes, block, tackle and kick a football for the glory of God. And off the field, I resolved that my language, my relationships with others, the books I read, the company I kept, everything would be done for the same reason. As the season wore on, I asked the coach one day if the entire team might pray before each game. Out of 100,000 boys in America who would have given anything to play this game, we had been chosen through the grace of God. Why not kneel before each game and acknowledge that fact?

In my second year something happened that thrilled and humbled me as much as anything in my career. I'd been selected to play in the annual Pro Bowl Game, and boys from every other National League team met together to practice. When the day of the big game finally came and we were assembled in the locker room, a boy from one of the other clubs said, "Dan, let's have a prayer."

I hope it's always clear that the purpose of my life is the acknowledgment of God.

Prayer

Dear Lord, take this day into Thy hands. Show me how each detail of the work I do may be made an occasion for acknowledgment of Thy goodness and mercy. I ask it in Jesus' name. Amen.

JIM RAY SMITH

Pride

Every one that is proud in heart is an abomination to the Lord. . . . PROVERBS 16:5

IT WAS DURING the exhibition season in the beginning of my second year with the Cleveland Browns—I was playing offensive left guard and still trying to get over that "on trial" feeling that every rookie has—when I injured my shoulder.

An alcohol rubdown, the infra-red lamp and a few hours of rest seemed to put the shoulder back in shape again. I played the first two games of the regular season with no problems. Then the shoulder started cutting up again. It was decided that two weeks of rest was in order. The first week was going along fine until I pulled a muscle at the end of the week. Then it broke loose— I was a "quitter," an "easy touch," a "softie," and a few other things that aren't mentionable. But the worst was to come. After being told off in no uncertain language, the coach ended with, "I guess we'll have to trade you or get rid of you!" This biting remark stuck in me like a knife. This was it. I was going home.

I called my wife in Dallas that night and told her I'd probably be home the next day. Then I went to my room and packed my bags. I felt I was through with pro football.

But before leaving, I knelt by my bed. Thoroughly discouraged and bitter, I asked God what to do. As I stayed there on my knees, it seemed that the mist suddenly lifted. I received an answer: *try one more week.*

Slowly I unpacked again, trying to comprehend this turnabout. Then I began to understand. No one had actually told me I was dropped from the team. I'd been bawled out just like a hundred, a thousand other men had been. I'd been ribbed and ridiculed just as almost everybody is at one time or another—and my *pride* had been hurt.

The next day when I showed up at the field, the man who'd read the riot act the day before apologized to me. "We've got a new deal for you, Jim," he said. "After that pulled muscle heals up, we're going to move you from left to right guard so you won't have to give that shoulder so much punishment!" I went into the next game at right guard and played the rest of the year there. I had a very good year. The following year I was moved back to left guard and I've been there ever since.

How can you protect yourself against every criticism, every unkind word, and carry your cross with Christ—both at the same time? It's impossible and the devil knows it.

Pride stands opposed to every advance in the Christian's life. Take the opening experience of conversion in which a man must admit his utter helplessness without Christ. Pride fights such a commitment. Take the act of witnessing about your new faith to others. Pride cautions against this because ridicule may result. Take the constant Christian exercise of putting others ahead of self—this is the very opposite of pride. Jesus said,

"If any man will come after me, let him deny himself, and take up his cross. . . ." Jesus made the cross a symbol of victory, but it is a victory achieved in humiliation.

Many Christians feel that in a moment of crisis they would be willing to lay down their lives for their faith. But how many would be willing to be spat upon, laughed at, held up to public scorn, ridiculed by enemies and deserted in shame by friends? And yet, when we consider that Jesus bore all this dishonor and more in order to secure our salvation, how can we justify our pride?

The struggle against this insidious enemy never ceases. Even when good habits establish themselves and our lives are free from the more obvious sins, the devil creeps in again. "You're living a life of real humility!" he says. "Congratulations!"

And there's pride again—pride in one's humility!

We need to keep coming back to the cross again and again to make sure the humility we display to the world is genuine.

Prayer

O God, keep me so close to my crucified Lord that pride can find no place in my life. Help me this day to carry my cross as a true disciple of Jesus Christ—in spite of ridicule or humiliation. I ask it in His name. Amen.

CARL ERSKINE

Dangers of Success

> Therefore let any one who thinks that he stands take heed lest he fall. I CORINTHIANS 10:12 (RSV)

> Neither be called masters, for you have one master, the Christ. He who is greatest among you shall be your servant; whoever exalts himself will be humbled, and whoever humbles himself will be exalted. MATTHEW 23:10-12 (RSV)

SUCCESS CAN BE intoxicating.

A boy nobody ever noticed before goes out for the high school baseball team and begins to hit home runs. Suddenly he is the "star" of the school. He is admired by the younger boys and treated with new respect by the boys who are older. Adults who used to look through him now nod and smile when they meet him on the street.

He looks in the mirror in amazement. He had always taken himself to be a rather ordinary person. But apparently he has been dead wrong. He is a very special guy. His walk becomes a strut. Condescension replaces courtesy in his manner. He begins to act as though the world owes him something.

I have seen this repeated in professional baseball. A rookie gets off to a tremendous start. The sports writers fill columns about his accomplishments. He is asked to speak before important business and professional groups.

Before long, his hat is much too small for his head.

It's easy to see how this can happen. In pro baseball it's possible for a talented boy to reach the top as a major leaguer in a season or two. It's enough to make anybody's head spin. A boy looks around and realizes that he is one of a small élite—450 baseball players to be exact—who are playing major-league ball.

He finds it a daily experience to rub elbows with other men who have reached the top in their professions—doctors, lawyers, teachers, and the others. But there's a difference. Most professional people spend a long time, including years of education, before real recognition. The baseball player can make it almost "overnight."

There's another difference too. He can be back in obscurity by this time next season if his batting average slips too far or an injury destroys his effectiveness. When this happens, the "overnight sensation" is often left with a bitter taste in his mouth and a sense of emptiness.

The only safeguard is an early realization that all natural ability is God-given, and therefore ought to be God-directed. ". . . let any one who thinks that he stands take heed lest he fall."

This realization can keep you steady at another time too—when you experience success. I've walked off the field after winning a big one, feeling pretty pleased about the applause and the congratulations. But when I've looked at the fellow in the locker-room mirror, I've been forced to say, "You little punk from Anderson, Indiana! You know you didn't do that!"

Deep in my heart, I know God has been responsible every time.

The measure of success I've had has made me feel humble. It has driven me to prayer. It's part of the reason I attend church regularly with my family.

Success is more than a gift. It is a sacred trust and a responsibility. If other people are looking at you because of your achievements, you must be careful. Your conduct will convince them either that you feel you deserve their admiration or that you realize your complete dependence upon God. I don't want anybody to find me basking in the glow of a compliment I know I really didn't earn.

What is "success" anyhow? Is it a high batting average, a fat bank account, a famous name? I don't think it is any of these things. A Christian is a "success" when he sees a purpose other than his own at work in his life and lines up with that other purpose.

A good friend of mine, Dr. Sam Shoemaker, tells of a woman he knows whose hip was broken when she was hit by a balloon tire that flew off a passing truck. He went to visit her in the hospital and found her in traction and in great pain. But she smiled at him and said, "I wonder what God has for me to do here!"

Dr. Shoemaker goes on to tell of the conversion of a nurse who read this woman's Bible to her each day and eventually caught her faith. In my estimation, this woman was a "success." I suspect that she would have been just as humble and true at the very pinnacle of what this world calls "fame."

Each of us can achieve this kind of "success" regardless of our vocation or position in life.

How about starting today?

Prayer

Heavenly Father, comfort us in times of defeat and discouragement. But keep us humble and prayerful when we enjoy what people consider "success." Lead us on to the real success that lies in following Thy will wherever it may take us. I ask it in Jesus' name. Amen.

FRANCIS TARKENTON

Complete Dedication

> Then said Jesus unto his disciples, If any man will come after me, let him deny himself, and take up his cross, and follow me. For whosoever will save his life shall lose it: and whosoever will lose his life for my sake shall find it. For what is a man profited, if he shall gain the whole world, and lose his own soul? MATTHEW 16:24-26

SOMEONE HAS SAID, "The devil can make a good man; but only God can make a Christian."

There are plenty of "good" people in the world. You meet them every day. They're folks who pay their taxes and try to keep out of trouble. As a rule they're friendly, reasonable and cautious. But God hasn't really gotten a hold on them. He's simply not real to them. He doesn't live in their lives. Strange to say, many have spent years in the service of the church. Some witness to a personal faith in Christ.

This was my condition. My father is a minister and I have known the church all my life. I'd made a commitment to Jesus as my Saviour and I wanted to do God's will. But I still saw the actual managing of my life as a personal responsibility. I had yet to discover the total way in which He can enter in and direct.

For example I thought that choosing a college was

something I had to figure out myself. As a senior in high school, I obtained information on the colleges that seemed interesting to me and drew up a list of preferences, first, second, third, and so forth. But as the time came near for decision, I was still uncertain.

One day Dad asked me if I'd prayed about the matter. I had to admit that I hadn't. A short time later, I went to my room and shut the door behind me. I knelt down and opened this department of my life to God. When I arose, the University of Georgia was in my mind as the clear answer. Interestingly enough, it had been third on my preference list before that prayer.

In spite of this and other experiences like it, I was still reluctant to give over to God all of my life until August, 1958, when I attended a Fellowship of Christian Athletes Conference at Estes Park, Colorado.

There I met and listened to some of today's outstanding athletes. I was impressed by the fact that they came from all over the country, freely contributing their time just to attend an FCA conference and share their faith in Christ. It made me feel pretty small.

At Estes Park I made a complete dedication of my life to Jesus Christ—with nothing held back. I told Him I would go anywhere, be anything He wanted me to be and do anything He wanted as He supplied the grace to do it.

Since then I have been thrilled to see Him moving in my life with new power.

In my junior year at Georgia, we were behind in the final seconds of an important football game with Auburn. We were on Auburn's 13-yard line and as quarterback I simply didn't know what to do next. I called time out and bowed my head in silent prayer. In that moment a play came into my mind that was brand-new. We'd never practiced it and I had to explain it in the huddle. But seconds later it broke perfectly and I fired a pass into the end zone for a 14-13 Georgia victory and the Southeast Conference championship. After all the shouting fans had left the stadium and the other players had left the locker room, I stayed behind to thank God for the play He had provided in answer to prayer.

I don't believe God promises success to everyone who becomes a Christian. And I don't think God "takes sides" in football games. But I believe He enables those who trust Him to do their best.

I saw this demonstrated again when I reported as a rookie quarterback to the training camp of the Minnesota Vikings. I had to memorize approximately 100 running plays and 100 passing plays. And when we came out of the huddle, the opposing team could shift into any one of ten or twelve defensive line-ups. These line-ups could cancel the play I'd called in the huddle and necessitate the immediate selection of a new play, a selection that had to be made in a matter of four or five seconds.

Time and again I came out of the huddle fighting the temptation to go blank. But repeatedly my silent prayer for help was answered by an inner calm and a cleared head.

I have come to know the truth of Philippians 4:13: "I can do all things through Christ which strengtheneth me."

If there seems to be something miraculous in the life of dedication, it is because there *is*. When a man gives himself completely to Jesus, Jesus gives Himself completely to that man. There's just one important thing to remember: the purposes of Jesus Christ are forwarded in the lives of His disciples—not in the purposes of the disciples. The power that Christ gives to those who trust Him can never be used for personal promotion. If success is granted, it is because He chooses to work that way. But He can work just as powerfully when His followers face defeat. He demonstrated this Himself when He was crucified as a common criminal.

Jesus is still calling disciples today. He is not looking for conventionally "good" people. He is looking for individuals who will dare to do His will—regardless of the cost.

Prayer

Dear Lord, challenge me to complete dedication to Your Son, Jesus Christ. Help me to dare to give over to Him the management of my life. Then show me how You can use victory and even defeat to Your honor and glory. I ask it in Jesus' name. Amen.

BOB PETTIT

The Church

> For by him were all things created, that are in heaven,
> and that are in earth, visible and invisible, whether they
> be thrones, or dominions, or principalities, or powers: all
> things were created by him, and for him: And he is before
> all things, and by him all things consist. And he is the
> head of the body, the church. . . . I COLOSSIANS 1:16-18

WHEN I PLAYED basketball my freshman year in high
school, I was the worst player on the team. I was too
slow and awkward, and in competition I was too rattled
to get off a good shot. Most of my time I spent on the
bench.

When we played away games, and there were too
many players for the one bus that was chartered, the
coach always picked me to stay behind. He knew my
absence from the game wouldn't hurt the team.

Even in home games I dreaded those moments in the
locker room right after the final buzzer. As the team
stripped for the showers, one boy would shout, "I got
ten points tonight. How many'd you get, Jack?"

And Jack would answer, "I got eight. But I missed
two easy ones!"

I'd hang my head and try to look as small as I could.
I didn't score a single point the whole season.

When I came out for basketball as a sophomore, my early season performance was so bad that I was cut from the team. My spirits hit rock bottom. In spite of a tremendous devotion to the game, I almost decided to give up.

But first I went to the pastor of my church in Baton Rouge, and poured out my disappointment. He listened through it all and then convinced me not to quit but to play on our church basketball team. It wasn't the greatest. In fact, most of the boys who played on it were rejects from the school teams, like myself. But we played hard and we played frequently. Sometimes during that season the same two teams in our tiny league faced each other twice or three times a week.

Little by little my confidence came back.

When I came out for high school basketball my junior year, there wasn't much argument about it. I was faster, more aggressive and a lot more accurate.

But I never forgot that the church saved my basketball career when it might have gone under without a ripple. And through the years I've come to learn that the church offers much, much more.

It provides a practical way for Christians to make a united impact on the society around them.

I've often heard it said that you don't have to go to church to be a Christian. But I can't understand how a true believer in Christ can ignore the fellowship Christ instituted to continue His work on earth.

A pastor once stood up to address a crowded sanctuary on Easter Sunday morning. "I want to wish you all a Merry Christmas," he said, "because I probably won't be seeing most of you again until then!" The challenge of a secular society will never be met by "Easter and

Christmas Christians." The church needs all of us, all the time.

As a youngster I sang in the choir. Later, I became an usher and served in other positions in my home church. I enjoyed every moment.

Now, when my career takes me away from home for much of every year, I often slip into an empty church in some distant city and commune there in silence. The architecture, the beautiful stained-glass windows and the familiar symbols of Christ's birth, death and resurrection all make me freshly aware of God and prompt me to worship.

But the "church" is not simply a building, a creed or a denomination. It's a fellowship of men and women related to each other in a common belief. How does that belief operate? Let me put it in basketball terms.

When I jump up to grab a rebound, I "believe" that nobody can stop me from getting that ball. There may be five other men pushing, shoving, jumping. I may be half crushed in a jungle of arms and legs. I may be off balance and late. But I'm in there "believing" and I'm convinced this is the secret of successful rebounding.

It is the secret of the church too. When we are united in our belief in Christ and His ultimate triumph, there's no force on earth or in hell that can stop us!

Prayer

Almighty God, I thank Thee for the many benefits I receive from Thy hand through Thy church. I thank Thee too for the opportunities to serve Thee that it provides. Keep me ready and willing to do my part in the great world-wide fellowship of those who love Thee. I ask it in Jesus' name. Amen.

FRANK BROYLES

Vocation

Now when Jesus was at Bethany in the house of Simon
the leper, a woman came up to him with an alabaster jar
of very expensive ointment, and she poured it on his head,
as he sat at table. But when the disciples saw it, they were
indignant, saying, "Why this waste? For this ointment
might have been sold for a large sum, and given to the
poor." But Jesus, aware of this, said to them . . . "Truly,
I say to you, wherever this gospel is preached in the whole
world, what she has done will be told in memory of her."
MATTHEW 26:6-10,13 (RSV)

Whatever your task, work heartily, as serving the Lord
and not men, knowing that from the Lord you will receive
the inheritance as your reward; you are serving the Lord
Christ. COLOSSIANS 3:23,24 (RSV)

GOD HAS A vocation for each of us. And sometimes it
turns out to be a surprise.

I wanted to be a professional football player from the
time I was eight years old. I practiced every chance I
had. I studied plays and went out for every team that
would take me. Then, in my last year of college, after
several good seasons, the break came. I signed up with
a professional football club. The contract was for a
salary that was bigger than anything I'd ever earned
before.

But an odd thing happened. A short time after signing, I was contacted by a school and asked to take a position with them as coach. The salary they offered was about one third that offered by the football club and there were a number of additional headaches. But I immediately applied for a release from the football contract. A few weeks later I was free to accept that coach's position and I did. I've been a coach ever since.

What happened was this: God revealed to me His plan for my life. I wasn't as clear about it then as I am now. But I knew I'd never be happy with anything else but coaching. Today I have a solid, deep-down feeling of satisfaction because I know I'm in the vocation I should be in.

I'm sorry for the athlete today who looks over several football, basketball or baseball offers and picks one just because it holds out the biggest bonus. I'm sorry for the boy or girl who picks a profession simply for its monetary rewards. Because they will spend the rest of their lives wondering about that "other" vocation, the one God might have shown them if they'd been willing.

"Christian vocations" are not limited to the ministry, mission work, and other church-related careers. I believe bricklaying, weather forecasting or clerking in a store can be "Christian vocations." It's *what we do* with the vocations we have that makes them secular or Christian.

Take a college football coach, for example. He can break his neck to secure the best players, overlook it when they break training rules, and play to win every game on his schedule, fair or foul. And he can excuse all his actions with the remark, "Football and God don't mix!"

But a coach who is a Christian will look at his vocation differently. He will tell you that his task is to build football players. To do this best, he must build men. The best example of manhood the world has ever seen was Jesus of Nazareth. Therefore he points his boys toward Him.

The Christian coach is interested in what his boys are doing before and after the game as well as what they do on the field. He wants to win games. But even more, he wants to create character.

This process of bringing Christ into one's vocation can be done in every field of human activity.

Here are three handy rules for making and keeping your vocation Christian:

1. *Keep Christ with you at all times.* You'll be surprised how this practice puts your vocation into focus—or leads you to change it. If you really take Christ with you, there are probably a number of places you just won't go any more. You'll be too ashamed to.

There will be quite a few things you won't say any more. You won't want Him to be present listening to them. And many things you won't want to do any more.

On the other hand, you may find yourself going places you were never interested in before—just because you feel He would want you to. And you may find yourself doing and saying things differently for the same reason.

2. *Be a good example.* What we *have* is a gift from God but what we *are* is our gift to Him. And this is our example before the world. "Whatever your task, work heartily, as serving the Lord and not men . . . you are serving the Lord Christ." If you take this verse seriously, people will begin to notice. And you will discover that it has nothing to do with the importance of your job as the world views "importance."

111

Once, when Jesus was visiting with some friends, a woman came to Him and anointed His head with some very expensive oil. His disciples objected to what they considered waste. But Jesus recognized the sacrifice involved and said, ". . . wherever this gospel is preached in the whole world, what she has done will be told in memory of her." It was a simple act, but it set a tremendous example.

3. *Win others to Christ.* This is the real "vocation behind the vocation" of every Christian. It should be said without apology. We are not here as Christ's disciples in the twentieth century just to make a fair living and die without debt. We are commissioned to spread the good news of the gospel.

When we do these three things, our vocations can be considered truly "Christian."

Prayer

Father in Heaven, help us to look to You for the special task You have for us on earth. May we receive our assignment gladly and try to find in it new ways to exalt Christ. We ask it in His name. Amen.

JOHN "Bubba" PHILLIPS

The Uncomplicated Life

Blessed is the man that walketh not in the counsel of the ungodly, nor standeth in the way of sinners, nor sitteth in the seat of the scornful.

But his delight is in the law of the Lord; and in his law doth he meditate day and night.

And he shall be like a tree planted by the rivers of water, that bringeth forth his fruit in his season; his leaf also shall not wither; and whatsoever he doeth shall prosper.

The ungodly are not so: but are like the chaff which the wind driveth away.

Therefore the ungodly shall not stand in the judgment, nor sinners in the congregation of the righteous.

For the Lord knoweth the way of the righteous: but the way of the ungodly shall perish. PSALM 1

. . . I have learned, in whatsoever state I am, therewith to be content. PHILIPPIANS 4:11

MOST PEOPLE BELIEVE they have to possess a lot of things to be happy. As a result, life gets pretty complicated. People who think this way never get enough.

That's because the only real satisfactions come from right living. I'm glad God revealed this to me early in my life. It has saved me from a lot of trouble.

I've tithed as far back as I can remember. I commit each day to God in prayer. And Sunday school and church have always had an important claim on my time. Even on the road, I do everything I can to attend church. In some cities like Kansas City and Washington, there are 9 A.M. services and I'm able to attend before reporting to the ball field. In other cities I attend on Sunday evening. During the winter when I'm driving long distances in the South scouting football talent, I keep my car radio tuned for gospel broadcasts. God has often given me guidance and encouragement this way.

I know that many people believe right living is dull and dreary. They just don't know. They've never discovered the joy that can be found in the simple things of life.

I wasn't born into a rich family. As a boy I sold watermelons, ran a paper route and worked in a local post office, to help out at home. And in between chores, I was out in the back lot in dungarees and a T-shirt throwing a football or baseball around—perfectly happy!

All my life I've been able to enjoy athletics, spend time in the out-of-doors and appreciate the beauty of nature. I've had good health and friends. These things are priceless and no amount of material possessions can replace them.

The greatest satisfaction, of course, is found in just doing God's will. Many times He will not provide you with the spectacular. Opportunities may seem pretty commonplace. But there is still pleasure in doing His will—whatever it may be. Living this way is rewarding in ways most people never guess. Added strength is provided for the problems of life that everyone faces sooner or later.

For example, a pitcher hits me at the plate once in a while. Sometimes it looks intentional. Maybe it is. But God provides me with patience and understanding. I pick up the ball and toss it back without a feeling of resentment. I realize the pitcher is working for a living too. Maybe he's feeling the pressure.

Then there's the poor season. My 1960 season was my worst in eight years of pro baseball. But I know that I was in every game, working offensively and defensively to the limit of my ability. And I was playing for the glory of God. Therefore the results are in His hands. I don't know what I'd do without this realization.

Sometimes there are tragedies in life that are really tough to take. My father was away from home on a business trip when he died of a cerebral hemorrhage. My brother was overseas in the armed forces. I was just a junior in high school. It was a terrific shock to everyone in the family. But I came to see that even circumstances like this are in His hands. Whether I understand them or not isn't really important, as long as I realize that He is in charge.

At one point in my baseball career, I broke my foot on first base trying to beat out a base hit. I was tempted to feel sorry for myself until I realized how many people were worse off than I. There's an old saying: "I complained because I had no shoes until I met a man who had no feet."

That's why I'm not complaining. Christ is everything to me. He has blessed me with a certain measure of success. But best of all, He has shown me that I can be happy with the simple things of life, the really important things.

I want to show my gratitude to Him by being a blessing to others.

Prayer

Lord God, thank You for life and health and the opportunities to do Your will wherever we are. Help us to find real joy in the basic things of life, even as Your Son did when He was here upon the earth. We ask it in His name. Amen.

DON DEMETER

Growing in Grace

> I am the real vine; My Father is the vine-dresser. He
> removes any of My branches which are not bearing fruit
> and He prunes every branch that does bear fruit to increase
> its yield. Now, you have already been pruned by My
> words. You must go on growing in Me and I will grow in
> you. For just as the branch cannot bear any fruit unless it
> shares the life of the vine, so you can produce nothing
> unless you go on growing in Me. I am the vine itself, you
> are the branches. It is the man who shares My life and
> whose life I share who proves fruitful. JOHN 15:1-5
> (PHILLIPS)

How DO YOU grow in this Christian life?

First of all, you can't grow if you've never been born.
Many people are trying to grow in the spirit who have
never been born in the spirit. This is hard work and
futile. Conversion is an absolute necessity. You must
become "a new creature" through faith in Jesus Christ.
This is the beginning.

But what then?

The Scriptures tell us that Jesus called His disciples
"that they might be with him." And in fellowship with
Him, they drew their strength. This is still the way
Christians grow. They grow in and through their fellow-
ship with Jesus Christ. This is not a static relationship.
It is dynamic.

117

As we move out in fellowship with Him to do His will, we find that even disappointments and difficulties help us to mature.

Many times during my baseball career, I've been tempted to be discouraged by setbacks. But God has made an occasion for spiritual growth out of each disappointment. ". . . The trying of your faith worketh patience" (James 1:3). I don't consider myself a natural-born orator. Far from it. Many times I've been tempted to back out of a speaking engagement in which I had an opportunity to witness for my faith. But I've been bolstered by God's words to Moses, "Who hath made man's mouth? . . . Now therefore go, and I will be with thy mouth, and teach thee what thou shalt say" (Exodus 4:11-12). Every time I have gone ahead in spite of my fears, trusting Him, I've been blessed. And I believe I've grown in spirit.

Through the years God has used certain people to help me grow. Bill Stevens, a lifelong friend of mine, is one such person. Bill was a Christian when I met him. His life and his family led me to the Lord. I saw in Bill's family what I wanted for myself—a family united in Christ.

In recent years I've been blessed through my friendship with Bobby Malkmus, a teammate on the Phillies club. When we're on the road, we often get together to pray and talk about the things in life that are most important. We have found the greatest power for our lives in the Word of God.

My wife Betty has been a strong influence for good in my life. During the four years of our marriage, we have read the Bible and prayed together nearly every day I haven't been out of town.

Both of us have Sunday school classes in the Exchange Avenue Church in Oklahoma City and when we're home, we enjoy discussing the lesson for each upcoming Sunday. One of the regrets I have about professional baseball is the fact that I miss out on the fellowship of the home church for part of every year.

Bible study is another important aid to growth as a Christian. All one winter in Oklahoma City, a group of us met each morning at seven in the Capitol Hill Baptist Church. Mrs. W. O. Merrill, an elderly lady who is a real student of the Scriptures, took us verse by verse through the Book of Genesis. We were two and a half months getting through it. Then we went on to Exodus. During that winter, I realized how little I knew about the Bible. I determined to spend the rest of my life in a systematic study of it. The whole experience of that winter helped me to grow as a Christian and to yearn for more growth. I am convinced that Christians would do more if they knew more of God's Word. If young people have trouble understanding the Bible, they must remember that it was written by men inspired by the Holy Spirit. This means that we must also be in tune with the Holy Spirit to receive its riches for our lives.

Prayer is still another means of growth. As we confess our sins to God, praise Him and make our petitions, we get to know Him better. We grow in our appreciation of His ways. We learn to pray things through until we have the answer or to wait in faith until He makes the matter clear.

One caution: some people feel that the Christian life is begun with a tremendous experience in which God "charges" us like a battery. Then we're on our own until we "run down." Prayer, witnessing, and Bible reading are thought of as separate exercises that "charge" us spiritually.

Actually our spiritual growth is "organic." It depends upon a vital, living relationship, day by day, with Jesus Christ. Jesus said, "I am the vine itself, you are the branches" (John 15:5, PHILLIPS). It's hard to think of a more organic kind of union than the vine and its branches. It suggests that as branches we draw our very life from the main trunk of the vine.

And what, finally, is the purpose of all this growing? "It is the man who shares My life and whose life I share who proves fruitful" (John 15:5, PHILLIPS).

Fruitfulness!

If we are going to be Christians, we want to be effective Christians. We want our life to count. We want to influence others to join us in discipleship. We want to make an impact on the secular world around us. We want to glorify God during the short time we have been given on earth.

We can only do this as we grow spiritually!

Prayer

Lord, give me a greater desire to live a dedicated Christian life. Make my fellowship with Thy Son a vivid reality in my life. Keep me in such union with Him in all that I do that I may experience spiritual growth and become more effective in my discipleship. I ask it in His name. Amen.

JACK PARR

Peace

Come to Me all of you who are weary and over-burdened and I will give you rest! Put on My yoke and learn from Me. For I am gentle and humble in heart and you will find rest for your souls. For My yoke is easy and My burden is light. MATTHEW 11:28-30 (PHILLIPS)

I leave behind with you—peace; I give you My own peace and My gift is nothing like the peace of this world. You must not be distressed and you must not be daunted. JOHN 14:27 (PHILLIPS)

May the God of Hope fill you with joy and peace in your faith, that by the power of the Holy Spirit, your whole outlook may be radiant with hope. ROMANS 15:13 (PHILLIPS)

PROBLEMS, ANXIETIES AND FEARS come to all of us. And there are just three things that we can do about them: (1) Try to relieve the pressure through anger, profanity, alcohol, drugs, and the like. (2) Bottle up everything inside. (3) Bring all the problems, anxieties and fears to the feet of Jesus and leave them there.

I have spent most of my life employing method #2.

I had problems at home but kept them to myself. I had concerns in school and anxieties about my athletic career too. But I put on a brave front and said nothing.

121

To make matters worse, I was overconscientious by nature. If the pot boiled over on the stove during dinner, I blamed myself for not taking it off the flame in time. If I got a B instead of an A in a subject, there was simply no excuse. And if our team lost a basketball game, the fault was all mine.

Success brought me no relief from tension. If we succeeded, I knew it was not because of my efforts. I tried extremely hard to live a good life. But I was always failing to meet my own high standards.

Long after the other boys had gone home following basketball practice, I stayed on, dribbling, shooting, rebounding. And late at night I'd come back and talk the janitor into unlocking the field house where I'd keep on practicing until 1 or 2 A.M. until I could hardly see the ball for weariness. In spite of this, I found it difficult to sleep. And when I did doze off, I'd wake in the morning as tired as when I'd gone to bed.

The pressures reached a climax in my senior year at college. I was taking a heavy load of subjects in pre-med and my marks were suffering. The chief reason was the long hours of basketball practice. Kansas State was ranked first in the nation in 1958 as we prepared for the big trip to Louisville to compete in the NCAA finals.

Sports Illustrated magazine predicted that if Jack Parr went to Louisville with the Kansas State team, we would win. As it turned out, we lost both games and in my mind, there was only one person to blame: myself.

I went back to college and a short time later suffered a complete nervous breakdown and was placed in a mental hospital. In severe depression and a frenzy of frustration, I tried to commit suicide. I cried out for God but I had made basketball my god and basketball couldn't help me.

In these black hours, I was visited by a minister from the University. At first all I asked was, "Why did this happen to me? I've always gone to church! I've tried as hard as I know how to be a Christian!" Then, little by little, I began to see the difference between "trying hard" to be a Christian and just "being" one through faith in Jesus Christ.

It wasn't sudden. I had a lot to think out. But in the hospital I had come to the end of my own resources. And this is always the place where Christ can be found —if there is a will to find Him.

I was in the hospital ninety days, a comparatively short period for a nervous breakdown. But Christ was already doing His wonderful work in me as I learned to give over to Him my anxieties about what people would say, my concerns for the future and all the other fears.

I went into professional basketball the year I left the hospital. I played with the Cincinnati Royals and enjoyed every minute of it. When I wasn't on the basketball court, I found myself reading the Bible more and more or discovering some of the rich treasures in devotional literature.

That same year I met the girl I was to marry and realized more clearly than ever how important it was for me to know Christ. I wanted Him to be the head of our family.

Since those trying days in 1958, I have come to know what it's like to lie down thoroughly tired and sleep soundly all night and wake refreshed. The difference is Christ and the peace He brings.

The Bible teaches that Jesus came to establish peace between God and man. The cross became the "bridge" over which men could walk and with their sins left there, enter into the presence of a holy God.

There is no peace like peace with God. It reaches to the center of your being and changes everything. No wonder Jesus could bid a cheerful farewell to His disciples with these words, "I leave behind with you— peace; I give you My own peace and My gift is nothing like the peace of this world."

Prayer

Dear Lord, I thank Thee for the coming into this world of Thy Son Jesus. I thank Thee that He lived and died on my behalf that I might experience forgiveness of sins and know a new life, freed of anxiety. Amen.

JERRY KINDALL

All for God

> Lord, what wilt thou have me to do? And the Lord said
> unto him, Arise, and go. . . . ACTS 9:6

> If our lives are centred in the Spirit, let us be guided
> by the Spirit. GALATIANS 5:25 (PHILLIPS)

> . . . I live; yet not I, but Christ liveth in me. . . .
> GALATIANS 2:20

MANY PEOPLE GET out their dedication like the family
Bible and dust it off once a week. They carry it to
church, then bring it home and leave it on the shelf
until the following Sunday. Other people carry it to
work where it influences their decisions and relationships on the assembly line and in the front office. Still
others feel that God should direct even the use of their
leisure time.

Just how far should we go with this matter of dedication?

"I beseech you therefore, brethren, by the mercies of
God, that ye present your bodies a living sacrifice, holy,
acceptable unto God, which is your reasonable service"
(Romans 12:1).

I believe that a careful reading of the New Testament will reveal that there are *no* special areas of a
believer's life that he can "run for himself." As a Chris-

tian, he has been "ransomed at a price," filled by the Holy Spirit, and is urged to offer his body as a living sacrifice.

Does it sound depressing? Does it sound as though the Christian ought to have some small area—perhaps an unimportant one—in which he can exercise his own will?

But what *is* "unimportant"? Can we ever be sure that we know?

Feeling discouraged after a batting slump in baseball seemed unimportant to me once. What could be more natural than feeling "down in the dumps" after striking out two or three games in a row? Then one day I thought twice about this and realized that in my dedication, I had reserved this little island of self-pity. I surrendered it and found that in the strength of Christ, I could rejoice and be thankful—even in a batting slump. Why not? Was His power and purpose in my life diminished by my failure to hit a baseball?

As the weeks and months passed, player after player approached me with words to this effect, "I've been watching you, Jerry. When you went into that slump a few weeks ago, I waited for you to blow up. But you didn't. I hit slumps once in a while too. I want to know how you do it." And time after time, there was an opportunity I would never have had otherwise, to tell another man about the Lord.

Today I have come to realize that Jesus Christ is capable of making every decision in my life. Nothing is too unimportant for His direction.

When my wife and I and our two children arrived in Mesa, Arizona, where the Chicago Cubs were to hold spring training, our first concern was the securing of a furnished house. It would have been natural to start through the classified ads, investigating each prospect on no other basis than our budget and our personal likes and dislikes. But prayer changed the character of this search. Instead of a routine chore, it became an adventure. Our goal: to discover the *one* place God had prepared for us.

After a patient, expectant search and looking to Him for guidance, we found it. And in the weeks that followed, in the neighborhood contacts, the friends met, the opportunities offered for witness, we saw some of God's reasons for choosing that house for us.

Is it impractical to pray about such things? Are we actually being unnecessarily "pious"? If we had picked the house ourselves, without prayer, couldn't God have blessed us in some other location just as well?

I don't believe so.

"The just shall live by faith." I take this to mean that the believer in Jesus Christ lives by quite another standard than the standards held in honor by the world around us. The world gives lip service to faith but is actually guided by common sense. Of course the Christian is not "against" common sense. He sees that it has a place, like the law of gravity. It is good as far as it goes. But it just doesn't go far enough.

The Christian has entrusted his life to Almighty God. This means his life joins the great mainstream of God's purpose as it sweeps onward to a grand climax somewhere in the future. It is impossible to examine such a surrendered life with as small a yardstick as common sense. Many times that life will seem to be doing something impractical or even downright foolish.

The Christian is simply marching to a different drum beat.

If anyone would know a victorious and happy life as

127

a follower of Christ, he had better not look back. He had better not reserve certain private areas of his life for his own tinkering and management. He had better decide to be a Christian "all the way."

Prayer

Dear Lord, help me now to make an unreserved dedication of myself to Thy Son. Help me to believe in His all-sufficiency and His willingness to live His life within me. Teach me moment by moment to depend upon His wisdom, His strength and His love. I ask it in His name. Amen.